W0008016

Rastafarian Mysticism

An Introduction to the Mysteries of Nyahbinghi

by
Ras Steven

INFINITY
PUBLISHING

Copyright © 2004 by Ras Steven

For information:
Ras Steven
PO Box 1383
Redway, CA 95560
or rassteven@starband.net

ISBN 978-0-7414-2071-8

Published by:

INFINITY PUBLISHING

INFINITY PUBLISHING
1094 New Dehaven Street, Suite 100
West Conshohocken, PA 19428-2713
Info@buybooksontheweb.com
www.buybooksontheweb.com
Toll-free (877) BUY BOOK
Local Phone (610) 941-9999
Fax (610) 941-9959

Printed in the United States of America
Published May 2013

This work is livicated to Queen Omega, the Feminine Aspect
of Divinity.

To my mother, Ellen; my wife Sharon; my sister Michelle;
and my friend Nitara

"King of Kings, Lord of Lords, Conquering Lion of the Tribe of Judah, Ilect of Thyself and Light of This World, InI Own Ivine Majesty Emperor Haile I Selassie I

JAH RASTAFARI"

Table of Contents

I. MYSTICISM: The Mystery Tradition

Many people around the world are drawn to Rastafari, sensing the Truth within, but are put off by the seemingly preposterous assertions of Rastas. The purpose of this work is to introduce and explain the major elements of the Rastafari Nyahbinghi Tradition from a mystical perspective and to demonstrate that it is a complete and usable Mystery Tradition. Emphasizing the pragmatic and experiential over the theoretical or dogmatic, these reasonings are offered as an aid to those who desire an overt intellectual understanding of the principles at play in the mystical experience of the Rastafarian ritual called Nyahbinghi.

Out of the mists of pre-history has come to us a tradition of exploring the Mysteries of life through the imaginative use of symbols. Imagination, being an integral part of humankind, has evolved along with us, and it is through this *image-making* faculty that we human beings have always approached the Mysteries.

Pre-dating the first cave etchings was the human imagination from which they sprang forth. Fourteen thousand years ago Neolithic humans crawled on their bellies with crude torches hundreds of meters down into the earth through torturous crevices to draw images on the wall there and then leave them behind enshrined in absolute darkness – why? Either they did this for their own personal edification or, more likely, to address unseen forces which they felt controlled their lives. Personal edification and harmonizing with the unseen forces of the universe are precisely the aims of mysticism. The existence of these ancient artifacts supports the premise that mystical urges have motivated humankind from time immemorial. Those drawings were expressive in nature and not materially functional.

Mystical impulses are a part of the human psyche. By 3000 B.C. humans had domesticated animals and developed methods of agriculture which led to communal living and the establishment of a civilized social order. From the outset the primary institutions were the temple and the government. Power was derived from fear. The fear that empowered established religion was of those aforementioned unseen forces. Ideas about those unseen forces have continued to develop apace with the human intellect.

The path of the mystic is one of initiation, myth, symbol and ritual. Mysticism is a process whereby the mystic makes fundamental changes within the psyche, so as to manifest and identify with the highest elements of the self. It is "the understanding that another faculty above reason is needed to guide human nature into union with the Divine..., when the existence and divine nature of the individual's own Higher Self is recognized". (Denning and Phillips, 1986)

The Mysteries represent quintessential truths which appear abstruse to the uninitiated. They are hidden in plain sight by the fact that they require a conscious act of imagination to comprehend. Reason is fully inadequate to the job of exploring the Mysteries. Like trying to taste a symphony or listen to a rainbow; a purely intellectual analysis of the Mysteries is misguided. Reason, as important as it is on its own plane, has a subordinate role in the mystical experience.

The Mysteries deal with realities for which common language is not suited, giving rise to the need for an elaborate system of symbols to express, discuss and even explore them. To one who does not approach a valid system of symbols with sincere openness to its influence, it will appear impenetrable, foolish or worse. Honest determination and perseverance however will yield initiation into a new mode of being.

The Greatest Mystery of all is referred to by the Rastafari as Jah, known variously to other cultures as God, Allah, Jehovah and thousands of other Names. Little can be said of Jah in literal language without running headlong into the wall of reason and descending into the quagmire of theological speculation and fundamentalism, so symbolic language becomes necessary. All of the venerable Mystery traditions have their own symbols and terminologies, yet they have more in common than not because it is the same Universal Truth to which they aspire. Every spiritual person will formulate a unique definition of Jah. This work will define Jah as Love; The Living Whole of Existence, the One Who Includes and Sustains All That Is and Is Not.

As soon as we speak of Jah, the ineffable Source and Sustainer of All, that ceases to be Jah, it is just a human idea. Like a taste bud trying to taste the tongue, the human psyche is essentially unable to conceive of Jah. This does not make Jah irrelevant, how can He Whose Essence We Are Of be irrelevant? Mysticism can put us in harmony with Jah, it cannot *explain* Jah.

The ancient maxim "As Above, So Below" succinctly explains the mystical conception of human nature and the universe. It is a formula which demonstrates that each human is a *microcosm* aligned with the universal *macrocosm*. This is to say that all of the forces at play in the universe are proportionally present within the human constitution. Exploring this formula with intellect, intuition and imagination will bring one to the mystical experience of the living reality behind the language. We realize that our own Higher Self is Divine, that at our core we partake of the Essence of Jah. It is by this direct perception that the mystic experiences Divinity rather than merely pleading to It from below.

Enlightenment, Divine Union, Nirvana, Self-Realization, Heaven, Mount Zion, Paradise, Gnosis, the Kingdom of Jah – many are the manifestations of the One Desire. The Mystery Traditions teach us that it is the goal and ultimate destiny of all life to resolve itself into its Source. Salvation is not a moment in time and Heaven is not a physical place. The Kingdom of Jah is an activity, a dynamic state of consciousness, eternally available only through the present moment. It is not an accomplishment so much as it is a mode of being. Enlightenment is an eternal becoming, an existence in accord with the dynamic dance of energies that is the Universe. All roads lead to Zion, all Mystery Traditions, including Rastafari, lead us to the act of letting go of the attachments of the lower self and of harmonizing our Higher Self with the vibrant flow of forces that constitute Creation. The idea of sacrificing the old self and being born anew recurs in many cultures across time and place.

Tradition, symbol, myth, sacrament and ritual are tools the mystic uses to stay focused on the One True Goal, but they are not goals in-and-of themselves. Most of the world's religious systems have a mystic tradition, but Jah is above all systems and traditions. Mystics must vigilantly guard against being corrupted by the ignorance of partiality and intolerance. We should never mistake the finger that points to the sun with the sun itself. This is why Mystics feel a kinship for one another which is above and beyond the constraints of religion, denomination and dogma. As His Imperial Majesty has taught us, "In the Mystic Traditions of the different religions we have a remarkable unity of spirit. Whatever religion they may profess, they are spiritual kinsmen. While the different religions in their historic forms bind us to limited groups and militate against the development of loyalty to the world community, the mystics have already stood for the fellowship of humanity ...in harmony with the spirit of the mystics of ages gone by. **No one should question the faith of others, for no human being can judge the ways of God.**"

There is in human nature a 'cycle of desire' which deludes us into chasing ghosts. Whether a particular desire ends in fulfillment or disappointment, it is inevitably replaced with a new desire. The Mysteries are about attending to the One True Desire; spiritual development is the only desire which will not ultimately disappoint. The mystic plainly sees that the inevitable destiny of humankind is spiritual evolution, just as the inevitable destination of a river is the sea. This evolutionary process is expedited by the self-transformational processes of mysticism.

InI Own Ivine Majesty Haile Selassie I JAH Rastafari

Self-transformation is the duty of the mystic. Haile Selassie I taught that "...we must look into ourselves into the depths of our souls. We must become something we have never been... we must become members of a new race". To be effective, the tools of tradition, symbol, myth and ritual must be vitalized with life force, energized by the Will through the Imagination. For instance, dreadlocks outside of Rastafari are a hair style, but within the mystical context of Rastafari dreadlocks become a living symbol of a spiritual commitment, an outward reminder of an inner reality.

Imagination is generally misunderstood and grossly underestimated. It is, as the word indicates, our image-making and image-perceiving faculty. It takes up where reason fails to comprehend the deeper meaning of symbols. Imagination does not reject paradox; it relies on an intuitive acceptance of Truth rather than on logical proof. The philosopher Iamblichus (250–330 C.E.), who extolled the virtues by which mankind obtains ecstatic union with the One, said that imagination is "superior to all nature and generation" and is that "through which we are capable of being united to the gods". Imagination allows the mystic to deal directly with the realities expressed by symbols without reducing them to language and running them through the filter of intellect. This is not a rejection of reason, but rather of its preeminence within the human constitution. Imagination will wander aimlessly and endlessly however, until brought under the direction of the Will.

The Will with which the mystic is concerned is akin to the 'will power' of the weight watcher. Will is an awesome power within humanity which is often atrophied by neglect. The practicing mystic strengthens the Will through exercise. Seemingly arbitrary rules of conduct within a tradition, such as dietary laws or other prescribed religious observances, serve to strengthen the Will of the aspirant. A strong Will can effectively guide the Imagination through the process of self-transformation.

The Mystery Traditions provide the Will with a tried and true map of guideposts left behind by others who have passed this way. This is why a tradition will work more reliably than a trial-and-error go-it-alone approach. This is also why an initiate is encouraged to stay on one chosen path until significant progress is made.

Initiation is an individual's introduction into a new phase of spiritual development, a new mode of being. Initiation is a personal transition, a death and rebirth. Often initiation is accompanied by a ritual and traditional instruction; self-initiation is slower and more difficult, but possible. An initiate has the subjective knowledge that he or she is fundamentally different than before initiation. This transformation embodies an organic commitment to the higher sphere into which one has been initiated and this commitment is the living reality behind whatever oath or vows are taken. Initiation is what the ritual of baptism and the myths of death and resurrection refer to. Ultimately, initiation is to be experienced rather than understood, a true Mystery.

Ethiopian priest at the portal of the 'Holy of Holies'

II. RASTAFARI: Roots and Culture

Before we can discuss the Mysteries of Rastafari a brief overview of the movement's history will be required to give context to concepts presented later. As we will see, the spiritual roots of Rastafari tap ancient sources; nonetheless, the seminal moment for the faith came in November of 1930 when Ethiopia crowned Haile Selassie I as Emperor with the official titles of King of Kings, Lord of Lords, Conquering Lion of the Tribe of Judah and Elect of God among others. Consequently, in the remote and impoverished nation of Jamaica, in a milieu of Africanized revivalist Christianity, emerged a new faith based on the divinity of Haile Selassie I, Rastafari.

Jamaica was originally inhabited by the Arawak Indians until the arrival of the Spanish in the early 16th century. The Spanish all but exterminated the Arawak and then imported slaves from Africa. In 1655, England took control of the island. Some of the African slaves of the Spanish took to the inhospitable mountainous regions of the island during the transition, where they lived secluded but free. The English consequently imported African slaves of their own.

Since Christian doctrine included the precept of the equality of all mankind before Jah, slave owners resisted disseminating religion among the slaves. As a result, whatever remnants existed of their various African religions were blended together and 'Kumina' arose as the slave religion of Jamaica. With the arrival of rivals to the Church of England from other Christian denominations throughout the second half of the 18th century and into the 19th century came the Christianizing of the slave population and their eventual emancipation in 1835.

These new Christians, with the lifeblood of African spiritualism still coursing through them, took quite naturally to the revivalist camp. Africanized versions of the Protestant

8

denominations became the predominant religious expression of the emancipated slaves and their progeny.

In 1914 Kingston, JA., Marcus Garvey organized the Universal Negro Improvement Association with his followers for the uplifting of Blacks everywhere. Garvey's visions were too radical for Jamaican society at that time and so he left for the United States in 1916. It is said that in his farewell address Garvey prophesied, "Look to Africa for the crowning of a Black king, he shall be the Redeemer." In Jamaica Garvey left behind a considerable following, the children of slaves who now saw Black dignity as a possible social reality, but lacked the leadership necessary to realize their vision. It was in this fertile soil that the seed of Rastafari first germinated.

It is historically unclear where or by whom the doctrine of Rastafari was first pronounced. Presumably, at least a few Garveyites and perhaps others would have formulated the concept of the divinity of Haile Selassie I upon learning of his wondrous coronation in Africa. Born Tafari Makonnen, this new emperor of Ethiopia took the name of Haile Selassie, meaning 'Power of the Holy Trinity'. In 1916, Tafari had received the title 'Ras', the highest rank outside the royal family (similar to a duke). No one knows why "Ras Tafari" was revealed as the 'New Name' instead of Haile Selassie or any other name or title held by His Imperial Majesty. But by 1934, centered in Kingston, Jamaica, the cult of Rastafari had emerged under the leadership of four individuals. These were Leonard Howell, Archibald Dunkley, Joseph Hibbert and Robert Hinds, each of whom claimed to have received directly and personally the revelation of the Black Messiah from the time of the coronation.

It should be noted that Rastafari as an organic grassroots spiritual expression has tended to be leaderless on the whole. Over the years different groups have formed and brought forth a call for centralization with differing degrees of success. However, "Rastafari has never been a

HIS IMPERIAL MAJESTY EMPEROR HAILE SELASSIE I

*"Look to Africa for the crowning of a Black king,
he shall be the redeemer"*

- *Marcus Garvey*

10

homogeneous movement. No formal organization unites all elements of the movement; no leadership hierarchy exercises control; and no established creed prescribes and ensures orthodoxy… [This lack of formal organization] allows the various Rasta groups and camps to enjoy a kind of freedom not always encouraged in many organized religions and secular movements." (Edmonds, 1998).

One prominent leader to rise up within the movement was Prince Emmanuel Edward, leader of the house of Rastafari called the Bobo. Bobo dreads always wear their locks tied up in turbans, often carry a broom to signify their cleanliness and hold Prince Emmanuel, called King Emmanuel posthumously, as a holy personage. Prince Emmanuel called the first Rastafari "Universal Convention" in 1958. Referred to as a 'grounation', this meeting with its drumming, chanting, banners and fire was the forbear of the powerful 'Nyahbinghi' ritual.

A central theme among the original or 'vintage' Rastas was repatriation; physically returning to Africa. It was their most immediate goal, a Garveyite dream, and until 1959 it was considered imminent. In that year another prominent leader named Reverend Claudius Henry deflated that dream by advertising a mass exodus of Black Jamaicans to Africa, supposedly at Selassie's behest, and started selling boarding passes at a shilling a piece. The long-awaited day arrived, hundreds of Rastas showed up packed and prepared and no ships or planes had been arranged. This fiasco was a hard-felt disappointment and has led to reformulations of the doctrine of repatriation.

In 1960, Mortimar Planno, a prominent Rasta, requested a study of Rastafari by the University of the West Indies. The University's report advised official tolerance of the legitimate faith of Rastafari and its recommendations to the Jamaican government won the Rastas irrevocable legitimacy within Jamaican culture. However, Rastas were still not well received by society at large and were persecuted. Scapegoated for the intense crime and violence

InI OWN IVINE EMPRESS MENEN – QUEEN OMEGA

of the early sixties, Rastas were routinely targeted by police, their enclaves and domiciles were raided and destroyed.

All of this began to change with the April 21, 1966 royal visit of Emperor Haile Selassie I of Ethiopia to the people of Jamaica. Thousands of Rastas flooded the airport and tarmac as a rainbow appeared in the cloudy sky from which the Emperor's plane descended. When His Majesty's airplane landed the police were unable to secure the airport. The Rastas were officially deferred to and Mortimar Planno was asked to help control the crowd and escort His Majesty from the plane. That day, for the first time, Rastas were invited into the halls of government as guests of honor.

Another important person in Rasta history is Vernon Carrington Gad, founder of the Twelve Tribes of Israel. This group made great strides in Rastafari's struggle for acceptance by recruiting membership from middle-class, educated suburbanites. The beliefs and practices of the 'Twelve Tribes' Rastas are progressive and show a distinct mystical element. Whites and women were fully accepted within the sect at a time when this was not considered orthodox by most Rastas. On the other hand, they are considered by some to be an authoritarian and elitist organization. Key to this group's success was the centrality of reggae music and the membership of superstar Bob Marley.

Robert Nesta Marley, born in 1945 at Nine Miles in the Parish of St. Anne, JA, became Rastafari's pre-eminent prophet. In 1961 his career was well on its way, but it was after Selassie's visit five years later that Marley's work showed a marked shift toward spiritual and social themes. The 1975 release of "Natty Dread" and an extensive world tour gained him international superstar status, but he was different from the typical pop superstar of the day. Entertainment seemed at times almost secondary to a spiritual mission to show the way of Rastafari to the world. Twenty years after his death Marley's work has become like musical scripture for Rastas; familiar comforting refrains which reveal ever deeper levels of meaning. Bob Marley was a member of the Twelve Tribes of Israel from 1975 until his death at age thirty-six.

In 1974, a coup in Ethiopia removed Selassie and it was less than a year later that His Imperial Majesty Emperor Haile Selassie I was reported to have died, although no body was offered as proof. This was a pivotal moment for a movement which tended to ignore death altogether. There was a remarkable lack of widespread shock. Some abandoned the faith and there was a momentary waning in the recruitment of new members, but the movement suffered no long term effect. Membership grew again, new groups formed, new myths appeared and the movement continued to thrive.

Today it is impossible to guess how many Rasta-farian enclaves exist worldwide, never mind how many individual Rastas there are. There are Rastas of virtually every race and nationality though the movement is predominantly Black. An ever-growing body of literature and regular assemblies from local to international in scope help to focus and define the movement as it continues to evolve exclusive of central authority. This lack of hierarchy means that there is no prescribed doctrine. Doctrinal development is not dictated by individuals but rather evolves organically as the movement grows; this is what InI refer to as the "Mystic Revelation of Rastafari". Some recent notable shifts within the movement include the de-emphasis of anti-white rhetoric, the rise of the Rasta woman and the intentional separation from dancehall and mainstream reggae pop culture.

The royal insignia of the throne of Ethiopia

III. SYMBOLISM: The Mystical Symbols of Rastafari

Mysticism deals with subjects not easily expressed in common language, it therefore relies on symbols. A symbol is an object which represents something else; commonly it is an emblem or sign which denotes something immaterial. In his book *Rastafari* Dennis Forsythe points out that, "A symbol can represent an entire philosophy through condensation and concentration. Symbols plumb depths which the intellect can see only obliquely... They provide the most effective and practical way of harnessing and using the creative power of the mind. A symbol is in fact the key through which man mentally makes contact with a particular quality which he desires to use. By this means internal transformation is achieved."

Human intelligence is symbolistic in nature. Very few of us ever find even a brief moment of inner silence; so what is it that disallows internal quietness? The 'noise' that rarely ceases is language, a system of symbols so entwined in human consciousness that the relationship between consciousness and language constitutes a mystery in itself. In fact, to contemplate anything that is not currently physically stimulating the senses is to employ symbolism.

Spoken language is sound symbolizing ideas and written language is glyphs, or drawn figures, representing the sounds of speech. Symbols can be simple and universal, like the solar disc, or very sophisticated and specific, like a royal insignia. The point, the line and the circle are the basic building blocks from which various alphabets are constructed and themselves represent pre-linguistic or archetypal ideas. In its most refined form, symbolism is employed where elaborate systems of symbols are used to direct the individual inward to the realization of the Unity of All.

It is well known that in the biblical tradition Jah created the heaven and the earth by use of language, "Jah

16

said, 'Let there be light" (Gen. 1:3) and that the messiah, called Jesus Christ, was the 'logos' or *Word* of Jah, "In the beginning was the Word, and the Word was with Jah and the Word was Jah" (John 1:1). This connotes the mystery of the relationship between language and consciousness and indicates that the individual's highest faculty is capable of creating its own world through the willful and imaginative use of symbolic language. Within Rastafari this Mystery is referred to by the formula "Word, Sound, Power".

The Rastafari, originating in Anglophonic Jamaica, have always sought to stretch the limits of language because it is widely recognized that 'The Queen's English' has imbedded in it a repressive vibration. For example, the words "understand", "wisdom" and "dedication" can be perceived to contain the negative vibrations of the words "under", "dumb" and "dead" within them. These negative vibrations serve to minimize or cancel out the power of the concept being expressed. The Rasta response to the negative influences within the Word Sound Power of the English language is to create a new form of linguistic expression, called *Iyaric* or Rasta speak, where the words mentioned above are transformed into "overstand", "wisemind" and "livication".

The most important and pervasive innovation of Rasta Iyaric is the conception and usage of the word "I". "I" is used in place of all personal pronouns so as to remove the illusory separateness of us/them and you/me and to consciously replace it with the concept of unity. "I" is worked into everyday speech as often as possible, continually invoking the spirit of "Inity" (unity). The "I" at the end of the written name "Haile Selassie I" is usually pronounced as the word "I" rather than as "the first" and quite often "I" is interjected between Haile and Selassie producing the potent Word Sound Power "Haile I Selassie I JAH Rastafari". The locution "I and I" or "InI" is used to express first the concept of 'me and my God' or 'my lower self and my Higher Self' and secondly it is used by an individual Rasta to refer to Rastafari collectively.

The musicality, the poetry, rhyme, innovation, rhythm and beauty of Iyaric within its native Jamaican patois is not easily reproduced. However, Iyaric is the language of the Rastafari and it is the responsibility of every Rasta to overstand its function and form and to use it inasmuch as their talent and natural disposition allow. Reciting biblical scriptures is a common practice among Rastas and it is customary to replace "the LORD" with "JAH" and to replace "me" and "us" with "InI" when reading or citing scripture.

This use of language not only provides cohesion within Rastafari and provides an effective means of communicating the Mysteries; it also actually begins the process of development within the individual by challenging one's fundamental perception of individuality. Changing language changes thought; changing how we think changes who we are.

Outside of language, the most visible symbol of the Rastafari is clearly the wearing of dreadlocks, although it is not always recognized that *not all dreads are Rasta and not all Rastas are dreads.* Dreadlocks carry symbolism which refers to two of the major doctrinal themes of Rastafari – Afrocentricity and the Biblical Tradition.

First and foremost, dreadlocks are worn to show that the Rasta has set himself apart from the ways of men and 'livicated' himself unto Jah. This symbolism derives from *Numbers* 6: 5, "All the days of their nazarite vow no razor shall come upon the head; until the time is completed for which they separate themselves to Jah, they shall be holy; they shall let the locks of the head grow long.", and is supported by *Judges* 13:5, "For, lo, thou shalt conceive and bear a son; and no razor shall come on his head: for the child shall be a nazarite unto Jah from the womb" and by *Leviticus* 21:5-6, "They shall not make baldness upon their head, neither shall they shave off the corner of their beard, nor shall they make any cuttings in their flesh. They shall be holy unto Jah and not profane the name of Jah". The primary translation of the Hebrew word 'nazar' is 'to separate', the nazarites were men or women who separated themselves from others by a vow of self-dedication to Jah. The biblical nazarite vow requires three outward signs of this inner commitment, they are (1) no drinking of wine or strong drink, neither partaking of any product of the grape, (2) the locks of the head are not to be trimmed but allowed to grow long naturally and (3) a nazarite must never come near a corpse. Samuel, Samson and John the Baptist were all nazarite locksmen; some Rastas cite Moses, David, Solomon and Jesus as dreads as well.

A Rasta called Iah C writes, "This dreadlocks (knots) upon I head and chin signify a difference and a distance between I and Babylon. The further into the woods or high hillside that man go the more natural man become, more ancient. The more conscious of Jah man is, the less man pay attention to false ego. Man who love Anciency find no delight in this modern world of vanity. The dreadlocks upon man head is the outer manifestation of the Covenant of Love made within man heart, between Jah and His Ancient servant, that man should live up to His Commandments, so that righteousness will cover the earth like water covereth the sea. Therefore I an'I dreadlocks is I an'I fullest physical reflection of the Love of the Living I." (*Jahug* vol. 2).

The wearing of dreadlocks within Rastafari began as an Afrocentric and specifically Ethiopianist impulse. Rastas believe that dreadlocks were worn by Ethiopian tribal warriors with whom they identify as spiritual warriors under H.I.M. Emperor Haile Selassie I. Adopting elements of Ethiopian culture is a way for Rastas to make a connection with their African roots and with Selassie. It also keeps alive the doctrine of the physical repatriation of the descendants of Jamaican slaves to Ethiopia and of all Blacks to Africa.

Probably the next most visible symbol of the Rastafari is the tri-color banner of red, gold and green. These are the colors of the Ethiopian flag and have been adopted by the Rastas. There are numerous interpretations of the symbolism of the colors. They can represent the three regions within Ethiopia, Tigre (red), Amhara (gold) and

H.I.M. displays the sign of Divinity's descent into the world

20

Shoa (green). Also, identifying Ethiopia with all of Africa as Rastas often do, the colors can be perceived to signify the blood of the African people, the wealth of the African continent and the fertility of the African land.

For Rastas, the colors symbolize the rainbow; the token of a Covenant between Jah and the earth (Gen 9:12, 13). And also that rainbow which encircles the throne of the Almighty from *Revelations* 4:3, "And he that sat was to look upon like a jasper and a sardine stone: and there was a rainbow round about the throne, in sight like unto an emerald". In fact, the conventional seven banded rainbow shows up frequently in the art of Rastafari as well.

One more place where color symbolism appears within Rastafari is in the attributions given to the twelve tribes of Israel. A system of correspondences has been created wherein for example Ruben relates to the color silver and the month of April, Naphtali to green and January and Joseph to white and February etc.

The six pointed Star of David, also referred to as the Seal of Solomon, is another important symbol. First it reminds Rastas of their direct link with the narrative of the Old Testament through their allegiance to the Throne of David from which Selassie ruled Ethiopia. The two superimposed triangles, one pointing up and the other down, represent the union of the opposites into one harmonious whole. They also represent Divinity descending to earth, the physical sphere, and Man striving and evolving toward Divinity as together establishing the Seal of the Covenant between them. In many of the photographs for which His Majesty posed, he held his hands together with the tips of his thumbs and forefingers touching in such a way as to form the downward pointing triangle of the Seal of Solomon. This pose is interpreted as a sign from Jah Rastafari Haile Selassie I that he is the Redeemer, the earthly manifestation of the Spirit of the Divine Whole.

Another of the potent symbols of Rastafari is the lion and again the foremost significance is biblical. One of Haile Selassie I's many official titles was 'Conquering Lion of the

Tribe of Judah'. Reference is made to that title in *Revelations* 5:5, "Weep not: behold, the Lion of the Tribe of Judah, the Root of David, hath prevailed to open the book and loose the seven seals thereof." The lion symbol has also an element of Africanism, Africa being home to the lion, and also an element of animism in that the animal itself represents power, pride and prowess. Many Rasta brethren consciously adopt the leonine characteristics of quiet strength and regal self assurance in their bearing and outlook. (Though some brethren seem to forget that Selassie taught us that strength must be balanced by mercy and ruled by love.) The lion symbol also adds another dimension to dreadlocks when they are seen as the Rastaman's mane.

Each of these symbols will continue to reveal deeper and deeper levels of meaning as they are studied and used as objects of meditation. Simply considering the history, the significance and the symbolism of each one, just exposing an open mind to its influence by spending time looking at it and thinking about it, allows the imaginative faculty to assimilate its meaning. In *The Rastafarians*, Leonard Barrett writes, "The symbol plucks all the strings of the human spirit at once, while speech is compelled to take up a single thought at a time. The symbol strikes at the most secret depths of the soul, while language skims over the surface like a soft breeze". (Barrett, 1997.) The logical reasoning faculty is not required here, it can help if it's well trained by the will, but usually its protests over being put on hold prove very disruptive to the process. This is where a Will, strengthened by determination and perseverance, can serve its master by restraining the intellect and allowing the symbol to directly inform the spirit.

IV. MYTH: The Mystical Truths of Rastafari

Myths are symbolic stories of our quest to experience life to its fullest, stories that hint at the spiritual potential of humankind. A story cannot rise to the level of myth unless its symbolic elements are integrated into a harmonious whole which refers to basic truths about the human experience. In order to operate as a myth the symbolic elements must also be generally meaningful to the intended audience; the more people who find meaning in the myth the more powerful it is. "People in traditional societies are all raised with mythological beliefs, and when these have not been tampered with they are the perfect structures for experience, revealing primordial truths to every epoch and race. They do their work beneath the surface of consciousness, instructing the soul on its origins, nature and destiny. Subtly they inform the mind, preparing it for the day when it no longer need be taught in parables."(Godwin, 1981.)

A story may be resplendent with white horses and black crows at every turn but if these symbols don't fit together there is no myth. However, if all the symbolic elements do work together, the story is not merely literally true, but is metaphorically valid; mystical truth. Hence we can read *Exodus* not as an historical travel log, but as showing the way out of mental slavery here and now.

It is by dealing with universal themes and archetypal ideas that myth appeals to the widest possible population. Themes such as birth, coming of age, parenting, self-realization, aging and death and ideas like mother, father, love, jealousy, pride, joy, sacrifice and fulfillment are the stuff of myth.

Myth is not less true than fact; it is symbolic rather than literal truth, but it is still Truth. Myth teaches us about life and dispenses the wisdom of how best to live it; it can lead us to the mystical experience of awakening to a spiritual level of consciousness in everyday life. The late sage Joseph

Campbell said, "The individual has to find an aspect of myth that relates to his own life... realizing what a wonder the universe is, and what a wonder you are, and experiencing awe before this mystery. Myth opens the world to the dimension of mystery, to the realization of the mystery that underlies all forms... If mystery is manifest through all things, the universe becomes, as it were, a holy picture. You are always addressing the transcendent mystery through the conditions of your actual world."

The mystical truth of Rastafari is the divinity of His Imperial Majesty Emperor Haile Selassie I, King of Kings, Lord of Lords, Conquering Lion of the Tribe of Judah, Elect of God, Light of This World, Earth's Rightful Ruler, JAH RASTAFARI. There are perhaps as many individual inter-pretations of this concept as there are Rastas, ranging from a fundamental belief that Haile Selassie is actually *the* God of the Old Testament Himself, to the belief that he is the returned Christ in His kingly manifestation. Some say that, like Jesus, Selassie is actually 'a priest after the order of Melchizedek', while other Rastas essentially see themselves as Christians and Selassie as man, prophet, teacher and Defender of the Christian Faith.

There are 'houses and mansions' within the movement, groups of Rastas who define themselves by sharing a particular dogma concerning Selassie. Some houses tend toward a species of orthodoxy and are intolerant of interpretations other than their own, while others are more liberal, open and tolerant. The movement derives strength from the freedom allowed by the absence of an authoritative hierarchy establishing canonical law and attacking dissension. The 'orthodoxy versus heresy' mindset that consumed Christendom has thus far been averted. As it is, all who hail His Majesty and adopt the symbols, myths and rituals of Rastafari can call themselves Rasta. A remorseless sinner will not be tolerated by true Rastafari, but within the parameters of the movement each Rasta will have his or her unique 'overstanding'. The Bible defines as righteous the one who is just and lawful, who "hath not oppressed any, but

24

hath restored to the debtor his pledge, hath spoiled none by violence, hath given his bread to the hungry, and hath covered the naked with a garment; … that hath withdrawn his hand from iniquity, hath executed true judgment between man and man."(Ez 18; 5-8). There is no tolerance for violence or dishonesty amongst InI. No one is perfect; however, a wolf among the sheep is an obvious danger and must be guarded against.

Selassie was alive less than 40 years ago and the Rastafari movement, much like the early Christian movement, is expressed by a rich diversity of sub-sects each with its unique exegesis. Bart D. Ehrman's book *Lost Christianities* tells us that, "In the second and third centuries there were Christians who believed that Jesus was both divine and human, God and man. There were other Christians who argued he was completely divine and not human at all. …There were others who claimed that Jesus was a flesh and blood human, Jesus, and a fully divine being, Christ, who had temporarily inhabited Jesus' body. …there were Christians who believed that Jesus' death brought about the salvation of the world. There were other Christians who thought that Jesus' death had nothing to do with the salvation of the world. There were yet other Christians who said that Jesus never died." This is not at all unlike the present state of Rastafari wherein no one interpretation has emerged dominant; many groups and individuals hold a wide range of beliefs about Selassie and yet they are still all Rastafari.

Three hundred years after the crucifixion the Christian movement was completely dominated by the Rome based Pauline sect, a self-proclaimed orthodoxy, and other groups were pronounced anathema and eradicated and their scriptures were proscribed and destroyed. Rastafari presents the world a new opportunity to establish a faith rooted in Truth and protected from corruption by the absence of an internal hierarchy.

It is still early in the life of the faith of Rastafari, even though its roots are ancient, and no definitive authority exists to establish a canon. There are the Bible, non-canonical scriptures, the biographies and utterances of Selassie, the histories of Ethiopia, Jamaica and the Rastafari and the contributions of many Rasta writers, poets and artists as well as many other ancillary sources from which each Rasta can construct their own vision of Rastafari. Immersing one's psyche in the mystical world of all the cogent symbols and myths of Rastafari, allows them to inform the soul directly, producing a positive effect which can be felt but not easily described. The Rasta have a saying, "who feels it knows it".

Below is a brief outline of the main mythological narrative from which the Rastafari draw meaning. This is one Rastaman's overstanding, acknowledging lack of expertise or authority and the many sources (remembered and forgotten) from which he has drawn inspiration. While centering on biblical themes, the whole Rastafari mythos cannot be seen there exclusively. One must seek out such sources as the *Kebra Negast*, the books of Enoch, the biography of H.I.M. Haile Selassie I, various non-canonical or alternative scriptures (e.g., *The Book of Jubilees*, *Gospel of Thomas*, Psalm 151) and Rastafari oral traditions, in order to piece together a cogent picture of the Rastafari mythos.

"In the beginning Jah created the heaven and the earth", so begins the great story. Having created the heaven and the earth, day and night, the waters and the dry land, Jah created man in His own image and likeness. Adam and Eve were the first man and woman. Jah made them to live in a wondrous place, Jah's garden called Eden. Adam and Eve lived there in perfect accord with creation until, tempted by Satan, a fallen angel in the form of a serpent, they disobeyed Jah and ate of the fruit of "the tree of knowledge of good and evil" which He had forbidden them to do (Gen. 2:9).

As a result of this 'original sin', mankind was cast out of paradise to toil for survival; "And Jah said, Behold, man is become as one of us, to know good and evil: and now, lest he put forth his hand, and take also of the tree of life, and eat, and live forever: Therefore Jah sent him forth from the garden of Eden, to till the ground from whence he was taken."(Gen. 3:22-3).

And it came to pass that man began to multiply on the face of the earth. Methuselah, son of Enoch, patriarch of the eighth generation of Adam, brought forth his son Nir to the people. "Here is Nir" he said "He will be in front of your face from the present day as a guide of princes", and then Methuselah died. The people accepted Nir as their priest before Jah, and he made sacrifice for Methuselah and glorified Jah. And the people of the earth prospered in the days of Nir for 200 years.

Then the people began to forget and turn away from Jah. Nir had grown old and his wife, Sopanim, was long past menopause and her womb had been ever barren. Yet Sopanim conceived in her womb in the time of her old age, though Nir had not slept with her nor any man touched her.

When Sopanim realized her pregnancy she became ashamed and hid it from her husband until one day very near the end of her pregnancy Nir summoned her. Nir saw her and he became ashamed and spoke harshly to her, saying "what hast thou done, wife, and hast shamed me before the face of these people" and "now depart from me" (*The Book of the Secrets of Enoch* 3:6). And it came to pass that when Nir did not believe his wife's account and told her again to "depart from me" Sopanim fell to the floor at his feet and died.

Nir was confused and afraid, so he went to his brother Noah to confide in him all that had happened. The two decided to bury Sopanim secretly and cover up the scandal of shame. They wrapped the corpse with black garments and prepared it for burial and went out to dig the grave in secret.

Shut up alone in the house, the child came out of the dead Sopanim. The child was as physically developed as a three year old and he was sitting on the bed next to his mother's corpse when Nir and Noah returned to collect the body for burial. They were very afraid. As they looked upon the child, they saw that the badge of priesthood was upon his chest and said "Behold, Jah is renewing the priesthood". Noah and Nir then took the child and dressed him in garments of the priesthood and called his name Melchizedek.

*And when those beasts give Glory and Honour and Thanks
unto HIM that sitteth upon the throne, who liveth for Iver
and Iver, the four and twenty elders fall down before HIM
that sitteth upon the throne and worship HIM that liveth for
Iver and Iver, and cast their crowns before the throne,
saying, 'Thou art worthy, O JAH, to receive Glory and
Honour and Power'*

In those days Jah saw that the wickedness of man had grown great and it vexed Him. Lawlessness, violence and corruption filled the earth. Jah said, "I shall destroy man, whom I have created, from the face of the earth".

Jah granted an apparition unto Nir and told him of the great destruction He had planned for the earth. And Jah assured Nir that He would send His archangel Michael to take the child Melchizedek and put him in the paradise of Eden. Jah did not allow Melchizedek to perish but rather established him as the priest to all holy priests, head of the priests of the future. Jah had established a priesthood in Melchizedek superior to the subsequent Levitical priesthood.

Noah also found grace in the eyes of Jah. Jah spoke unto Noah and told him of the great flood that was to come and Jah instructed Noah in the construction of an ark, a giant boat, aboard which would be preserved Noah and his family and two of every living thing of all flesh; male and female. Then all the fountains of the great deep were broken up and the windows of heaven were opened and every living substance was destroyed which was upon the ground.

After the water receded, Noah and his three sons Shem, Ham and Japhet and their wives re-peopled the earth. And the whole earth was of one language, and of one speech. It came to pass in the time of Nimrod, grandson of Ham, that the people conspired to build a brick tower "whose top may reach unto heaven". Jah realized that having one language the people, acting as one, would have the power to do anything they could imagine and Jah saw that man was not yet ready to use this power wisely. So Jah confounded their language that they may not understand one another's speech and He "scattered them abroad from thence upon the face of the earth; and they left off to build the city".

Many generations later, we have Abram, who as a young man worked for his father selling icons and statues of household gods. One day, alone on the road carrying a bag full of his father's wares, he was struck by the wonder and beauty of the setting sun and stopped to rest. He took the idols out of the bag and lined them up on the road and demanded of each that it prove itself. As each god failed to answer him Abram kicked it over in the dust. And when none were left standing, Abram looked up at the wonder of the sunset and the grandeur of All and cried out for Jah. Jah heard Abram and answered him, "Now Jah had said unto Abram, Get thee out of thy country, and from thy kindred, and from thy father's house, unto a land that I will show thee". (Gen. 12: 1)

Living where Jah had directed him, in the plain of Mamre, some years later, Abram received word that his brother Nahor was taken captive in war. He armed his household and trained servants and pursued his brother's captors. Abram vanquished Chedorlaomer, king of Elam, and the kings that were with him. He returned triumphant to Jerusalem with all of his brother's household and the spoils he had won.

Upon his return to the city Abram was blessed by Melchizedek, King of Jerusalem and priest of Jah. And in return Abram awarded Melchizedek one tenth of all he had as tithe. It was this blessing from Melchizedek which prepared Abram to become Abraham, the father of a multitude of nations. Then Jah made His Covenant with Abraham and his seed after him; that He will be their God and they His people.

Abraham's son Isaac bore twin sons called Esau and Jacob. Jah had informed Isaac's wife that she would bear the twins and that they shall be two nations and that the elder shall serve the younger. The firstborn, Esau, came out red and hairy with his brother firmly grasping his heel. Esau grew to be a hunter, a man of the field, while Jacob was a plain man. One day Esau came in from the field feeling faint and wanting food, thinking quickly, Jacob offered to buy Esau's birthright for some bread and lentils – Esau foolishly accepted the terms.

When Isaac was upon his deathbed he asked Esau to go out and hunt a deer and to prepare his favorite venison dish saying that after eating it he would give Esau his blessings. Isaac's wife Rebekah overheard their conversation and while Esau was out hunting she quickly prepared the dish with meat from a goat. She disguised her favored son Jacob so that he would appear as his brother to the aged and dying Isaac and sent him to deceive his father and receive the blessings Isaac had intended for Esau. Jah allowed Rebekah's scheme to succeed so that Jacob did receive the blessings.

Jacob was later visited by Jah in a dream and Jah renewed the covenant He had made with Abraham with Jacob and his seed. Jacob went on to sire twelve sons; Reuben, Simeon, Levi, Judah, Issachar, Zebulun, Joseph, Benjamin, Dan, Naphtali, Gad and Asher. Jah told Jacob, "thy name shall not be called any more Jacob, but Israel shall be thy name" and his twelve sons became the patriarchs of the "Twelve Tribes of Israel".

Of all his sons, Israel loved Joseph the youngest best of all and this made his brothers jealous. Making matters worse were the visions Joseph had which seemed to imply that his eleven brothers would bow down before him; visions which Joseph shared aloud with Israel in earshot of his brothers. Consequently, acting more or less of one accord, his eleven brothers conspired to leave Joseph for dead in a hole in the ground. They spattered his clothes with animal blood and brought them to Israel as 'proof' of Joseph's demise at the claws of a wild animal. Israel was deceived and moved by a great grief.

Joseph was rescued from the pit by merchants who sold him to slave traders who in turn sold him into bondage in Africa. Joseph had the gift of interpretation of dreams and, because Jah was with him, whatsoever Joseph became involved in prospered. This remarkable slave soon came to the attention of Pharaoh, who made Joseph ruler of all the land of Egypt, second only to the Pharaoh himself.

Then a great famine swept across all the lands, for which Egypt alone was prepared because of Joseph's wisdom. Canaan was sorely afflicted and Israel sent his sons to go and ask for famine relief from Pharaoh. When they arrived in Egypt they brought their petition before Joseph as

31

Pharaoh's representative and they did not recognize their own brother whom they had betrayed. Joseph forgave his brothers, as Esau had forgiven Jacob, and Israel moved to Africa where they survived the famine and prospered.

As generations passed and Pharaohs came and went, Israel thrived and increased in Egypt. This did not escape the notice of the native Egyptians who responded by putting Israel into bondage.

It was after many generations in slavery that Jah caused a deliverer to be born to Israel. Moses was born during a time when the Egyptians were attempting to further weaken Israel by killing all of their sons at birth. Moses was spared because his mother hid him for three months and then set him afloat in the Nile wherefrom he was plucked by the daughter of Pharaoh. She made Moses her own son and he was raised in the house of Pharaoh; educated by the best teachers and initiated by the high priests.

When Moses was grown he came to know of his true heritage and he looked upon the bondage of his brethren. One day he saw an Egyptian beating a Hebrew and Moses killed the Egyptian and hid his body in the sand. But soon the story of Moses' deed started spreading and he left Egypt.

Moses took an Ethiopian wife and settled down keeping his father-in-law's flocks until Jah heard the cries of His people and He answered. Jah spoke to Moses from out of a bush consumed by fire yet not burned. And Jah charged Moses with the responsibility of presenting His ultimatum to Pharaoh, "Set my people free". Moses protested that he was unequal to the task and certainly not a gifted speaker. Jah insisted that Moses act and granted that his brother Aaron may accompany him and even speak for him.

Jah worked many wonders and miracles through His servant Moses. After numerous confrontations, threats and plagues, Pharaoh acquiesced to let Israel go free. But soon Pharaoh had second thoughts and set out to cut down Israel even after giving them leave. Jah granted Moses the power to drown the armies of Egypt in the Red Sea. Thus was Israel liberated from bondage and free to go now to the

Promised Land, the land 'flowing with milk and honey' where they would establish themselves as a nation.

It was during their exodus through the desert that Moses received the Law. Moses left the encampment to go alone upon Mount Sinai and to commune with Jah. Jah said, "Come up to me into the mount, and there I will give thee tablets of stone, and a law and commandments which I have written; that thou mayest teach them" (Exodus 24:12). Moses received much instruction from Jah, including the 'ten commandments', many laws of conduct, both secular and religious, and directions for the construction of the 'Ark of the Covenant'. Also called Zion, this was to be the earthly habitation of Jah, to be housed in a tabernacle and to be ministered to by a high priest.

The people of Israel grew impatient waiting for Moses to return. They forgot Jah and all He had done for them and they doubted Him. "When the people saw that Moses delayed to come down out of the mount, the people gathered themselves together unto Aaron, and said unto him, 'Come, make gods for us, who shall go before us; for as for this Moses, the man that brought us up out of the land of Egypt, we know not what is become of him" (Ex 32:1). Hence they caused Aaron to construct false gods of his own design and he made offering upon their altars. Jah grew angry with Israel and threatened to wipe them from off the face of the earth and to establish His nation anew through Moses, but Moses interceded. He prevailed upon Jah to remember Abraham, Isaac and Jacob and to forgive the weakness of their children. Moses then returned to his people hot with anger and rebuked them soundly, destroying their golden calf god and teaching the laws of Jah.

Obeying the word of Jah, Moses caused an ark (an elaborate chest) to be built to very exact specifications. Jah told Moses, "thou shalt put into the ark the testimony which I shall give thee". Also constructed according to the exact instructions given by Jah was the tent, or *tabernacle*, in which the ark would reside and all of the furnishings thereof, as well as the complete set of garments and vestments to be worn by Aaron and his sons who shall serve as priests unto the Ark.

When all of the preparations were correct and complete, Moses erected the tabernacle tent with all of its furnishings and accoutrements. Then he placed two stone tablets bearing the Ten Commandments which he had received from Jah in the Ark of the Covenant and moved its lid into place. This lid was itself a wonder to behold; a slab of gold measuring approximately four feet by one and one half feet, with a winged cherub at either end facing center, all cast as one piece. The space between the winged angels, or *cherubim*, was called the "mercy seat" or "seat of mercy"; it was from here that Jah spoke unto the priests of Israel. "And there I will meet with thee, and I will commune with thee from above the mercy seat, from between the two cherubim which are upon the ark of the testimony, of all things which I will give thee in commandment unto the children of Israel." (Ex 25: 22). Moses then covered the Ark with a veil and installed it in the Holy of Holies, the inner sanctum of the tabernacle.

When all of the work was done according to the will of Jah, a cloud covered over the tent and the glory of Jah filled the tabernacle. "When the cloud lifted from the tabernacle, the Israelites would set out on their various journeys but if the cloud did not lift, they would not set out until such time as it did lift. For over the tabernacle a cloud of Jah rested by day, and a fire would appear in it by night, in the view of all the house of Israel throughout their journeys." (Ex 40:36-8).

In time, as promised, the Israelites were led to the land of Canaan, but not before the death of Moses. Because of the golden calf incident, Jah made Israel to wander for forty years in the desert so that none of those who belonged to that generation would live to see the Promised Land. Jah blessed Israel and soon they became a great nation in that land. And again the people turned aside and forgot their Covenant with Jah, they corrupted themselves with foreign gods and evil dwelt in their hearts. Jah rebuked them by delivering them into the hands the Philistines for forty years.

During the Philistine occupation Samson was born and the Spirit of Jah was with him from the beginning. "And there was a certain man of Zorah, of the family of the Danites, whose name was Manoah; and his wife was barren, and bore not. And the angel of Jah appeared unto the woman, and said unto her, Behold now, thou art barren, and bearest not: but thou shalt conceive and bear a son. Now therefore beware, I pray thee, and drink not wine nor strong drink, and eat not any unclean thing: For, lo, thou shalt conceive, and bear a son; and no razor shall come on his head: for the child shall be a nazarite unto Jah from the womb: and he shall begin to deliver Israel out of the hand of the Philistines." (Jud 13:2-5).

Samson was a mighty warrior for Israel, single-handedly killing a thousand Philistines once with the jaw bone of an ass. Jah had hidden Samson's strength in his dreadlocks; a secret which he foolishly divulged to his unworthy Philistine wife Delilah. She betrayed him and caused the Philistines to "cut off the seven locks of his head; thus she weakened him and made him helpless" (Jud 16:19). Samson was captured, but Jah still granted Samson his great strength one last time, allowing him to topple the two center columns of the temple of Dagon where the Philistines had tethered him. "Samson cried, 'Let me die with the Philistines!', and he pulled with all his might. The temple came crashing down on the lords and all the people in it. Those who were slain by him as he died outnumbered those who had been slain by him when he lived." (Jud. 16:30).

Later, in the time of the prophet Samuel, the Israelites began to petition Jah through Samuel that He should establish a monarch for Israel. Now Samuel also was a nazarite since the time before his conception when his mother Hannah prayed, "O Jah of hosts, if thou wilt indeed look on the affliction of thy handmaid, and remember me, and not forget thine handmaid, but will give unto thy handmaid a man child, then I will give him unto Jah all the days of his life, and there shall no razor come upon his head." (I Sam 1:11). "The word of Jah was rare in those days; visions were not widespread", yet Jah spoke to Samuel from the 'mercy seat' on the Ark of the Covenant. The people of Israel prevailed upon the prophet to petition Jah for a king to rule over them. And Jah warned the people through His prophet that a king would take their sons for war and their daughters for cooks and tax their fields and orchards and livestock, "And ye shall cry out in that day because of your king which ye have chosen you; and Jah will not hear you in that day". Still the people insisted they wanted a king to rule over them such as the other nations had, and Jah relented, saying to Samuel, "Hearken unto their voice, and make them a king".

Samuel took a flask of oil and poured some on the head of Saul, kissed him and said, "Jah herewith anoints you ruler over His own people". King Saul led Israel in their fight for independence from Philistine rule, and it came to be then that the Philistines had amongst them a giant warrior named Goliath before whom all of Israel was afraid; all but one meek shepherd boy who was steadfast in Jah and said, "Who is that uncircumcised Philistine that he dares defy the ranks of the Living God, Jah?" (I Sam 17:26).

With only a sling and a stone, the shepherd boy David challenged Goliath, "Thou comest to me with a sword, and with a spear, and with a shield: but I come to thee in the name of Jah, the God of the armies of Israel, whom thou hast defied." (I Sam 17:45). David slew Goliath and as a result the Philistines were routed.

David became famous and beloved of the people of Israel and this vexed Saul sorely. When Saul died David was made King of Israel. He was a good king and led his people in many victories. When David took Jerusalem he brought the Ark of the Covenant into his new capitol and consolidated his authority. "Thus David and all the house of Israel brought up the Ark of Jah with shouts and with blasts of the horn." (II Sam 6:15).

36

*"He shall build an house for My Name, and I will stablish
the throne of His kingdom forIver."*

           -    *II Samuel 7:13*

Before David died Jah spoke to him through the prophet Nathan saying, "When your days are done and you lie with your fathers, I will raise up your seed after you, one of your own issue, and I will establish his kingship. He shall build a house for my name, **and I will establish his royal throne forever**." (II Sam 7:12). Thus Jah founded the Throne of David upon the earth for all time.

In the fortieth year of his reign David had his youngest son Solomon anointed King of Israel and then died. Solomon was a great king; he was blessed by Jah with unsurpassed wisdom. Solomon built a magnificent temple to enshrine the Ark. He was beloved of all his people and his reputation reached across the whole land.

In Ethiopia, the Queen of Sheba, Makeda, heard of Solomon's wisdom. Like many other rulers, Makeda wanted to meet Solomon, witness his kingdom and learn from him. She made the journey to Jerusalem and did meet King Solomon.

Sheba was greatly impressed by what she saw and she devoted herself and her kingdom Ethiopia unto Jah, the God of Israel. Solomon was smitten by Makeda's radiant and majestic beauty and he cunningly seduced her. Makeda, the Queen of Sheba, returned to Ethiopia with Jah in her heart and the son of the King of Israel in her belly.

Makeda carried the child to term and bore Solomon a son in Ethiopia, he was called Bayna-Lehkem which means "son of the wise man". When he was grown Bayna-Lehkem journeyed to Jerusalem to meet his father and receive his blessing. Solomon not only gave his blessing, but anointed Bayna-Lehkem King of Ethiopia with the name King David II; he was also called Menyelek I in Ethiopia. "Then his father Solomon the King also said unto Zadok the priest: Make him to know and tell him concerning the judgment and decree of Jah which he shall observe in Ethiopia." (*Kebra Negast*).

When Menyelek departed Israel he took with him a new royal court composed of the children of Israel's priests, officers and councilors. "And then they prepared their children to send them into the country of Ethiopia, so that they might reign there and dwell there forever, they and their seed from generation to generation." Menyelek and the sons of the nobles departing for Ethiopia did also take with them the Ark of the Covenant. "And now Jah hath chosen thee to be the servant of the holy and heavenly Zion, the Tabernacle of the Law of Jah; and it shall be a guide to thee forever, to thee and to thy seed after thee. For thou wilt not be able to take it back even if thou wishest, and thy father cannot seize it, for it goeth of its own free will." (ibid.).

After the tragedy of having lost the Ark, Solomon fell from grace. Overly distracted by his sexual appetite, his wisdom dissipated. His sons who ruled after him proved to be inept and soon the children of Israel were scattered over the earth and their 'promised land' was occupied by various invaders over the centuries.

In the first century of the Common Era, Rome occupied Palestine. The Jews there had a precarious relationship with the Romans, who were somewhat more tolerant of the Jews than other regimes had been. Within the Hebrew community, two groups were vying for dominance over the religious life of Jews; the strict Pharisees with their own oral traditions regarding observance of the law and the Sadducees of the traditional ruling class of priests. And it was into this setting that Yeheshua was born in Nazareth, his mother was called Mary and she was blessed by Jah and her husband Joseph was of the lineage of David. Yeheshua was also a nazarite, as was his cousin, John the Baptist, who prepared his way among the people.

Yeheshua, called Jesus in Greek, had the Spirit of Jah with him. He was a great teacher and healer; he worked miracles to emancipate mankind from the mental slavery of sin. Despite what was said of him, all available documentary evidence indicates that Jesus considered his own mission to be the spreading of the 'good news' of salvation, the coming of the 'Kingdom of God'. He transformed himself that we may be transformed; he showed the way.

It is difficult to discuss Jesus in strictly rational terms without crossing the line between reason and mystery. And to present any one interpretation of Jesus as objectively authoritative is presumptuous, divisive and sometimes dangerous.

The Christian myth contains elements which are of the highest order of mystical truth; capable of leading the individual to a richer life experience. Unfortunately however, it also has woven into it elements which are repressive, guilt-based and life-denying and have yielded hatred and perversion in Christendom. (The Rastafari shall never forget that the bombs with which Mussolini massacred defenseless Ethiopians were personally blessed by the Roman Catholic pope.)

During the first centuries after the death of Jesus, many different sects of Christianity sprang up, each with a different interpretation of Jesus. There were most notably the Ebionites, the Marcionites, various Gnostic congregations and the Pauline sect which attached itself to Rome. It was this Pauline sect which used its affiliation with Rome to become the 'orthodox' religion from which all of our modern denominations of Christianity derive. The Roman Catholic Church is a relic of the Roman Empire and has been administrated under the same authoritarian model. Once a certain interpretation of Jesus was adopted by the Roman cult, all other interpretations were pronounced heretical, viciously suppressed and ultimately eradicated. Consequently, most of what modern Christians consider to be the unshakable tenets of their faith were interjected by men long after Jesus' death. Dogma such as the virginity of Mary, the authority of the priesthood, the denial of reincarnation, Jesus' role as the one and only mediator between man and Jah and even the very divinity of Jesus are among the many tenets that were injected into the Christian faith by those who dominated it many generations after the crucifixion.

By using brutal methods which were in direct and obvious contradiction with the teachings of Jesus, Christianity spread itself across the western hemisphere with atrocious violence. Over the subsequent centuries many offshoots from the original Roman cult have taken root; remnants of the various other Christian sects of the first two centuries, however, are sparse.

In Ethiopia, "Between the 10th Century B.C. and the 4th Century A.D. there was the merging of SEMITIC immigrants with the Cushite (Black African) inhabitants which produced a new culture and civilization known as the AKSUMITE Empire, and a new language called GE'EZ evolved. The Aksumite Kingdom reached its zenith in the 4th Century during the reign of King EZANA."

"KING EZANA was the 4th Century King of Aksum during whose reign Christianity was introduced to Ethiopia. He conquered the Nile Valley Realm of Kush (Meroe) and extended the frontiers of his Kingdom. He ascended the Throne between 320 - 325 A.D. and introduced the title of 'KING OF KINGS'."

"King Ezana received a Greek and Christian education from a Syrian Christian named FRUMENTIUS, who was employed by his father, King ELLA AMEDA, and who also became co-regent. Around 333 A.D., Frumentius was allowed to go to Alexandria in Egypt to obtain a Bishop for Ethiopia. The Patriarch of Egypt, named Athanasius, consecrated Frumentius himself as the first Bishop of Ethiopia, under the name of ABBASALAMAI (Father of Peace). First to be converted, King Ezana became Protector of the new religion." (Alemu, 1994 p.3-4). The Solomonic line of kings remained on the throne of David in Ethiopia, with few interruptions, until the reign of Haile Selassie I, the 225th descendant from King Solomon.

It was on the 23rd of July, 1892, in the region of Ethiopia called Harar, amidst a terrible drought that Tafari Makonnen was born and the heavens opened up and poured forth life giving water and the earth was satisfied. "Thou, O Jah, didst send a plentiful rain, whereby thou didst confirm thine inheritance, when it was weary."(Ps. 68:9). The Spirit

Tafari Makkonen age 12

of Jah was with Tafari from birth. He was ordained a deacon at age eight; at eighteen he became governor of Harar and at twenty-four Ras Tafari was appointed regent and heir to the throne. In 1930 he was crowned Emperor Haile Selassie I, King of Kings, Lord of Lords, Conquering Lion of the Tribe of Judah, Root of David, Seed of Solomon, Elect of God, Light of the World. He is also called Power of the Holy Trinity, Earth's Rightful Ruler, Wonderful Counselor, King Alpha and Queen Omega, Ancient of Days, Abbabajanoi and The Almighty I, JAH RASTAFARI.

The accomplishments of this noble and exalted man are far too numerous to mention them all; here is a brief list of some of them: he gave Ethiopia its first written constitution, its first printing press, its first airplane and airline, its first domestic modern hospital and its first university, he abolished slavery, he co-founded the Organization of African Unity, he traveled the world and received many degrees from prestigious institutions of learning around the globe, and he held Ethiopia together through Mussolini's vicious invasion and brief occupation of Ethiopian territory. He was a venerable man, a great leader and a teacher by example; a selfless and enlightened man of Jah.

Like Christianity, Rastafari has more power and importance as mystical truth than as accurate historical fact, though both faiths do have historical elements. Perhaps this is because, like Jesus, Selassie represents a Mystery of the highest order with significance too great to be comprehended by the human mind at this time.

For the Rastafari, Selassie is a manifestation of the Most High Jah; *the* manifestation for InI in this time. He is InI spiritual focal point – JAH RASTAFARI. And InI are His chosen people, the modern day Israelites who inherit and stay true to the spirit of the Covenant that Jah made with Abraham, Moses, David and Solomon.

Prince Makkonen, as young regent of Harar Province, Ethiopia

V. RITUAL: The Nyahbinghi

This life, the life you find yourself in right now, is all that you have. And it is in this life that you can discover the Mysteries. What is required is not a new life, it is a new way of experiencing this life. Ritual gives us a way to experience our life which can open us to the transcendent which is always all around us and of which we are a part. Manly P. Hall explained, "Life is the great mystery, and only those who pass successfully through its tests and trials, interpreting them aright and extracting the essence of experience therefrom, achieve true understanding. Thus, the temples [of the ancients] were built in the form of the world and their rituals were based upon life and its multitudinous problems." (Hall, 1998)

Mystics will interpret everything that life presents symbolically, mythologically and/or ritually, thereby linking themselves to a whole which is greater than any individual consciousness. Any menial task, from washing dishes to lighting incense, can be ritually performed by being wholly present in the moment, mindful of the significance of the act (both literal and symbolic) and attentive to the connection being made with all who have performed this act throughout history. They must be aware, as aware as possible, of their every action, thought and feeling in every aspect. By focusing on the true and highest meaning of the act and subduing all dissonant actions, thoughts and feelings, awareness can slip away leaving only being. The actor disappears and there is only action. Here, in this moment, is a mystical experience, where the lower self is suspended and a new level of consciousness is awakened to. Moments such as these leave an indelible mark upon the psyche, as the Higher Self informs the lower.

Organized ritual concentrates and intensifies this process by setting apart time and space for this purpose and by the addition of other participants. Setting apart time

45

provides relief from the demands of everyday life. And setting apart a space allows the creation of an atmosphere designed to facilitate the ritual through the selection and arrangement of the most potent and relevant symbols. The addition of more participants increases the amount of energy or life-force behind the intention of the ritual.

Ritual is symbolic behavior, mystical action; it is not so much a means-to-an-end as it is an end-unto-itself. Ritual is not rational behavior it is expressive in nature, by expressing qualities or ideals one intentionally installs them into the psyche. So, for example, by focusing on the ideal of kindness, concentrating on it internally and acting on it externally one will become, in time, more kind. This process can be further facilitated by surrounding oneself with others who share the same intention and with appropriate symbols, while avoiding all sources of energy which do not resonate with the intention being expressed.

Israel Regardie, in his book *The Tree of Life* wrote, "Each individual part of man, each sense and power must be brought within the scope of a rite in which it plays a part. It is our preoccupation, normally, with the separate perpetual requirements of the body and mind and emotions which blind us to the presence of that inner principle, the sole reality of the interior life. Hence one of the requirements of ritual is that it must either fully occupy or tranquilize those particular portions of one's being that the transcendental union with the [Divine] may not be interfered with."

Experience is the key. The mystic knows that no symbol or group of symbols truly expresses the reality of mystical experience. Symbols merely suggest the truth; it is through ritual that one actually partakes of the Mysteries. As Joseph Campbell said, "A ritual can be defined as an enactment of a myth. By participating in a ritual, you are actually experiencing a mythological life. And it's out of that participation that one can learn to live spiritually."

Participants intentionally don a mythological or ritual role within the context of a rite. Using symbols, language and physical actions with attentive inward focus, the participant puts aside the individual self and steps into the ritual role. The individual suspends personality and acts from the role, just as a judge in robes in the courtroom is expected not to make judgments based on personal feelings and opinions but to act from the role of judge and make judgments based on the law.

Ritual is an important part of Rastafari, both in the context of the mystical interpretation of everyday life and in the context of formal rites. Each Rasta mystic conducts his own life ritualistically; studying scripture, smoking herb, wearing locks, praising His Majesty and remaining diligently focused on the manifestation of Jah Love through his being. The supreme ritual of the Rastafari is called "Nyahbinghi", where Rastas come together to invoke Jah Love, praise the Almighty and fight against all evil conceptions of mankind with the weapon of Word Sound Power of Jah Rastafari. The next chapter will focus on the mystical/ritual approach to daily life which the Rasta call "livity", while this chapter will examine the Nyahbinghi ritual.

The origin of the word 'Nyahbinghi' is unclear. It may have come from a religious anti-colonial movement from turn of the century Eastern and Central Africa. Jamaicans first became aware of the term when, during the ramp up to the invasion of Ethiopia, the fascist Italian propaganda apparatus circulated a photograph of Haile Selassie wearing a traditional lion mane headdress with the story he that he was the head of a secret society called the 'Nyahbinghis', an international African conspiracy to overthrow white colonial governments around the world; they said that the word Nyahbinghi translated to mean "death to the whites".

Today 'Nyahbinghi' can refer to the Order of the Nyahbinghi, to the ritual Rastafari gathering or to the drums used at the ritual. The accepted definition of the word is "death to white and black downpressors" (oppressors); 'death' here refers to Divine intervention and not to violence at the hand of man. Nyahbinghi Rastafari fights oppression spiritually and non-violently.

photograph of His Majesty wearing a lion mane headdress circulated by Italian fascist propagandists

The Nyahbinghi Rasta Elder Bongo Thyme said, "And herein, The Order of the Nyahbinghi is an Ivine Priestly Order. It was originated and originally used by Melchizedek the High Priest and King of Righteousness. And was resurgent in these ages by the Rastafari brethren who are the blessed children of the King of Righteousness". (*Jahug*, vol. 2.) The Ancient Nyahbinghi Order, also referred to by such titles as 'Order of Melchizedek Nyahbinghi' and 'Theocracy Reign Ivine Order of the Nyahbinghi', is the most mystical/religious House of Rastafari, its roots reach into the depths of ancient history. This is a most serious and sincere mystical Order and should not be taken lightly.

A Binghiman knows InI to be the modern Israelites, the chosen few, we who minister unto the Almighty Jah in the Rainbow Circle Throne Room, nazarites livicated unto Jah and initiates of the Order of Melchizedek. InI are here as Jah warriors to fight this Armageddon with jubilant chants and blazing drums, proclaiming Judgment and calling out to Jah for victory over all evil conception. "These people have I formed for myself, they shall shew forth My praises" (Isa. 43:21). "...for he is the Lord of lords, and King of kings: and they that are with him are called, and chosen, and faithful" (Rev. 17:14).

There is a trinity of drums in the family of drums called Nyahbinghi. First there is the bass drum, referred to as the *'pope-smasher'*, which is a large hoop-style drum headed on both sides with animal hide. It looks much like the bass drum of a marching band and is played with a mallet. The bass drum is the grounding point of the ritual, it manifests the heartbeat of Creation and is the foundation upon which the other drums and the chants rely. Next is the *fundeh*, a cylindrical drum 1'-3' tall with a goat hide head usually 9"-11" in diameter on top and open at the bottom. The four steel rods which are used to secure and tune the head are extended at the bottom of the drum creating legs which keep the bottom rim from setting on the ground and

a Rasta altar

Nyahbinghi drums

dampening the sound. The fundeh plays the main rhythm of the Nyahbinghi chants. Finally there is the drum called the 'repeater' or '*peater*, sometimes called the *kete*, which is exactly the same in design as the fundeh. Though it is generally smaller, the repeater really only needs to be tuned higher than the mid- to- low tuning of the fundeh. The repeater plays a syncopated melody over and interlaced with the rhythm of the fundeh and the melody of the chants. The repeater part is improvised by an experienced drummer of stable and non-partial character who is ever conscious of the whole of the circle and responds to the spirit of the moment, working to facilitate the efficacy of the ritual for all participants. During the ritual only one kete plays at a time so as to augment and ornament the chants and avoid distractions.

As mentioned before, the "Universal Convention" called by Prince Emmanuel Edward in 1958 is commonly cited as the first Nyahbinghi, though undoubtedly smaller Rasta gatherings had taken place previously and developed at least some of the elements of the ritual celebrated today.

The Patriarchs of the Ancient Nyahbinghi Order in Jamaica have established and forwarded a set of guidelines "so that InI brothers and sisters be aware of the commitments one has to abide by to be a true Nyahbinghi Rastafari". Following these guidelines as closely as possible, groups of Rastas worldwide are able to found their own Houses which can sponsor Issemblies on the Hola days.

While some Rastas live fairly isolated lives, away from 'Babylon' (i.e., the rat race; 'the ways of man'), others live within the mainstream culture. Some Rastas are able to assemble weekly for Sabbath or more often, while others come down from the hills only for Nyahbinghi. Rastas have a saying, "iron sharpen iron" which expresses the need for coming together; it means that Rasta strengthens Rasta. There are several 'Hola days' (holidays) in the Rastafari calendar upon which Nyahbinghi Issemblies are called:

January 7 – Ethiopian Christmas
April 21 – Emperor Haile Selassie I's visit to Jamaica

May 25 – African Liberation Day
July 23 – Birth of Tafari Makonnen (Haile Selassie I)
September 11 – Ethiopian New Year
November 23 – Coronation Day.

The Nyahbinghi Order in Jamaica celebrates these events for seven days and nights. The House also honors February as Black History Month, Ethiopian Liberation Day on May 5th and Marcus Garvey's birthday August 17th.

The Nyahbinghi grounds, the site on which the gathering is held, centers on the Altar, which should be housed in a Tabernacle. The centerpiece and focal point of the Altar is a portrait of His Majesty. The Altar is draped with red, gold and green coverings; herbs, scriptures, fresh fruits and vegetables, frankincense and other appropriate symbols and offerings (such as Coptic crosses, incense, flowers etc.) are placed around the portrait. Every Rasta must approach the Altar and give thanks and praises to The Most High.

The Nyahbinghi Fire is to burn unceasingly throughout the Issembly. It is best if the Fire is central and visible from within the Tabernacle. The Fire is lit and tended by one Fire Man and his choice of help. It is prohibited to throw anything but pure clean wood into the Fire. The Fire symbolizes the destruction of evil; it is seen as a Hola Fire unto the Creator Selassie I Jah Rastafari. The Fire Man is a ritual role invested with authority and should be performed by a principled Rastaman of balanced mind. At the same time, every Rasta is a Fire Man; it is a matter of duty to keep Jah Hola flames of judgment and purification burning internally, eternally.

Aside from the Tabernacle and Fire, the grounds must provide space for rest, food preparation, child care and sanitary conveniences. It is helpful if the setting is natural, so that the senses are limited to seeing, hearing, smelling, tasting and feeling sensations which arise only from the ritual and Nature.

Coronation Day November 2, 1930

It is the serious responsibility of all 'sons and daughters' trodding the Issembly to abide in perfect love and harmony. Discordance of all kinds is prohibited; lying, slander, greed or unfairness shall not be tolerated. Sexual behavior is prohibited during Nyahbinghi to facilitate the meditation of holding all brethren and sistren in undifferentiated impartial regard; one perfect love. Other observances expected at Nyahbinghi include no meat, no drugs or alcohol, that only men play the *harps* (drums) and that men wear their locks uncovered, while women cover their heads and wear dresses, befitting their royal dignity.

Rastafari is undoubtedly patriarchal, as have been most Biblical traditions. The presence and power of the Rasta woman has yet to achieve its fullest manifestation. Apparently, vintage Rasta brethren openly prevented women from attaining any significant standing within the movement. Now there are houses such as the King Alpha & Queen Omega Theocracy Daughters, to encourage and promote the development of respect, knowledge and the spiritual powers of the Rastafari woman.

The ideal to which Rasta women aspire is that of Empress Menen, Haile Selassie's loyal and dignified wife; interpreting her as "Queen Omega", the feminine aspect of the Most High Jah. Still, the roots of the movement are male oriented and as a result a number of the ritual practices at Nyahbinghi reflect this tradition. Women are not to administrate around the Altar nor play the harps and are expected to avoid Nyahbinghi Issembly during menses.

While the movement does seem to be evolving toward a less male-dominated model, it must be allowed to evolve organically from within. To take liberties with ritual, to accept some elements and reject others, is to disrespect tradition. Summarily altering the precedents, precepts or principles of the ritual unilaterally would be presumptuous and not an acceptable response to any perceived limitations of the tradition. The Mysteries of Rastafari mystically reveal themselves and it is upon this Mystic Revelation of Rastafari that InI rely to right all wrongs in the fullness of time.

EMAYE (Dear Mother) Empress Menen

The Rastaman owes respect to Woman, "Queen Omega", mother- sister - daughter - wife, without whom the Manifestation of Creation would be impossible. "And there appeared a great wonder in heaven; *a woman clothed with the sun*, and the moon under her feet, and upon her head a crown of twelve stars" (Rev. 12: 1).

Although there is no ostensible hierarchy of authority within the Nyahbinghi, respect for elders and tradition is expected. Also, a necessity arises for a kind of priesthood within the ritual, to administrate around the Altar, read scripture, lead the congregation in prayer and generally see to the orderliness of the ritual. The role of Nyahbinghi priest is for brethren who lead exemplary lives in the sight of the congregation and the Almighty, they must be just and non-partial Rastafari. The role of the drummers is also of great import, they are the angelic harpists, the players of instruments who attend the Circle Rainbow Throne, "And I heard a voice from heaven, as the voice of many waters, and as the voice of a great thunder: and I heard the voice of harpers harping with their harps: And they sung as it were a new song before the throne" (Rev. 14:2, 3).

With the opening of the Tabernacle the Nyahbinghi begins. All in attendance gather at the Tabernacle facing east before the Altar and the priestly brethren lead the congregation in reciting Psalms (1-7, 121, 122, 133, 24) and the Nyahbinghi Creed;

> "Princes and Princesses must trod out of Egypt, Ithiopians now stretch forth their hands to JAH, O I JAH of Ithiopia, InI own Ivine Majesty. Thy Irits [Spirits] trod into InI hearts to dwell in the paths of righteousness, lead InI. Help InI to forgive that InI must be forgiven. Teach InI love and loyalty as it is in Mount Zion. Endow InI with wisemind, knowledge and Iverstanding to do Thy Will O JAH Ras Tafari. Thy blessing unto InI O JAH; *Let the hungry be fed, the naked clothed, the sick nourished, the aged protected*

and the infant cared for. Deliver InI from the hands of InI enemies that InI must prove fruitful in these perilous days when our enemies are passed and decayed, in the depths of the sea, in the depths of the earth, in the belly of a beast or in the lake of fire. O give InI a place in Thy Iverliving Kingman. This I ask in Thy Great and Thunderable Name Haile I Selassie I JAH Ras Tafari. Through the power of the King of Kings, Lord of Lords, Conquering Lion of the Tribe of Judah, Ilect of Thyself and Light of this World, InI own Ivine Majesty Emperor Haile Selassie I, First Ancient King of Creation. JAH art the Alpha and Omega the beginning without end, First and ForIver, the Protectorate of all Iman faith and the ruler of the Iniverse. So hail I JAH and King Emperor Haile Selassie I JAH Ras Tafari! Almighty I JAH Ras Tafari!! Great and Thunderable I JAH Ras Tafari!!!"

The "Fire Key" is lit with the reciting of Psalms 68, 2, 83, 94, 20, 11 and 9 and the Hola Fire is kept burning for the duration of the ritual. Then the harpists begin to play and the Nyahbinghi chants (songs) rise up from the congregation. Between and during the drumming and chanting, spontaneous voices call out to the Name of Jah, or cry out Judgments such as "Fire burn!" and "Red hot!" The drumming and chanting can go on all day and/or night. It is common for the Ises (praises) to go up all night by the firelight with the daytime spent resting, cooking and eating and reasoning. 'Reasoning' is discussing and exploring any aspect of Rastafari in depth, especially scriptural and theological themes.

Participants are expected to assume the ritual role of the Nyahbinghi Rastafari in its fullest mystical manifestation. InI become pure Sons and Daughters of the Most High rallying around the Rainbow Circle Throne, giving praises to His Glory and calling down Judgment upon wickedness;

here to establish "Theocracy Reign", Jah's Government on earth which shall rule Creation in Love, Purity, Holiness and Unity with Affection, Compassion and Humility. In this role each Rasta remains steadfastedly rooted in full awareness of Jah Love throughout the ritual, not only when giving praises around the Altar, but even during private moments, when reasoning, while cooking, at meal time etc.

Another quote from the Rasta writer Ras Iah C eloquently expresses the essence of the ritual role of the Nyahbinghi Rasta; "When one love Jah with intensity one do everything one do just to please Jah. So material world flee further away. Jah love-spell soon free up man to chant Jah name and give Jah thanks an' praises without fear of persecution an' ridicule. The greatest deed man can do is praise His Imperial Majesty without apology. InI a natural man. Natural woman. During Iyahbinghi Issembly, InI reveal true heart love for Haile I by jumping and chanting higher. Triumphant! Beat harps fiercer than man of lesser faith. O what a roaring thunda InI utter from out of InI mouth. When Binghi Ises go up InI enthusiasm for InI Creator put InI inna trance. Transform InI flesh into a divine temple of love of the Almighty I Jah Rastafari. In such a trance, overcome with joy, InI excel and exceed the mundane world of physical sense gratification." (*Jahug*, vol. 2.)

Surrounded by the living ritual of Nyahbinghi, all one really needs to do is step aside and allow the Mystery. Trying too hard can be a trap, it creates tension and self-awareness. Having an intellectual understanding of the ritual beforehand is most helpful, but at ritual the intellect itself is a distraction. The adept becomes comfortable putting the personality, the lower self, to sleep. Relaxing into the ritual-self is very much like falling asleep in that effort is counterproductive. Like sleep-consciousness, mystical-consciousness naturally arises when waking-consciousness fades under the appropriate circumstances. The process of suspending waking-consciousness, of intentionally but effortlessly putting aside the lower self and calmly accepting a new mode of consciousness must be practiced and experienced to be understood.

A key element of the Nyahbinghi ritual and of Rastafari as a whole is the use of the hola herb called ganja, Irie, Ishence, kali, kaya, the weed of wisdom; marijuana. The subject of marijuana is the focus of much sensationalism. Many books, essays and articles on the subject can be easily found both for and against it. The history of, the many uses of, the cultivation of, the botany of, the chemistry of, the laws regarding and the social politics of this plant are all worthy of note, but not relevant here. The present discussion will be limited to the mystical properties of and use of herb within the context of the Mysteries of Rastafari.

"And Jah said, Behold, I have given you every herb…" (Gen. 1:29), the Rasta belief in the use of herbs is grounded in the Bible. "Better is a dinner of herbs where love is, than a fattened ox where hatred is" (Pro. 15:17), "He causeth the grass to grow for the cattle, and herb for the service of man" (Ps. 104:14), "And the angel of Jah appeared unto Moses in a flame of fire out of the midst of a bush" (Ex. 3:2), "And the angel shewed me the river of the water of life, clear as crystal, flowing out of the Throne of Jah and of the Lamb through the middle of the street of the city. On either side of the river was there the Tree of Life, which bare twelve manner of fruits, and yielded her fruit every month: *and the leaves of the tree are for the healing of the nation*" (Rev. 22:1-2); these are important passages cited by Rastas to illustrate their relationship with the herb. Many Rastas say that the herb grew in the Garden of Eden, that the 'weed of wisdom' was found growing at the grave of King Solomon and that ganja was the 'new wine' which the apostles claimed they were 'drunk' on at the Pentecost. Many Rastafari will also assert that the presence of the ganja tradition was intentionally and maliciously expunged from the Bible by unscrupulous translators.

The following remarkable text is from the *Book of Enoch the Prophet*, a 'lost book of the Bible' rediscovered in

Nyahbinghi Blessing at 'Reggae On The River' 2004

the author at Issembly

Ethiopia in 1773; "Among these there was a tree of an unceasing smell; nor of those which were in Eden was there one of all the fragrant trees which smelt like this. Its leaf, its flower, and its bark never withered, and its fruit was beautiful. Its fruit resembled the cluster of the palm. I exclaimed, Behold! This tree is goodly in aspect, pleasing in its leaf, and the sight of its fruit is delightful to the eye. Then Michael, one of the holy and glorious angels who were with me, and one who presided over them, answered, and said: Enoch, why dost thou inquire respecting the odour of this tree? Why art thou inquisitive to know it? Then I, Enoch, replied to him, and said, Concerning everything I am desirous of instruction, but particularly concerning this tree. He answered me saying ...And that tree of an agreeable smell, not one of carnal odour, there shall be no power to touch, until the period of the great judgment. When all shall be punished and consumed for ever, this shall be bestowed on the righteous and humble. The fruit of this tree shall be given to the elect. ...Then they shall greatly rejoice and exult in the Holy One. *The sweet odour shall enter into their bones*; and they shall live a long life on the earth, as thy forefathers have lived; neither in their days shall sorrow, distress, trouble, and punishment afflict them. And I blessed the LORD of Glory, the everlasting King, because He has prepared this tree for the saints, formed it, and declared that He would give it to them." (Charles, 1896.)

In his paper *African Dimensions of the Rastafarian Movement,* Neil J. Savishinsky has stated that "in certain regions of Africa cannabis is employed by religious groups that are, for the most part, "expressive" in nature – those wherein individuals seek to change themselves or their external environment through processes involving possession, meditation, dance, and the ingestion of psychoactive substances". (Savishinsky, 1998.) The Rastafarian ganja tradition could be a revived fragment of African religious life. However, African Jamaicans were certainly introduced to ganja by Hindu Indian laborers early in the twentieth century.

Dennis Forsythe states in *Rastafari* that "Rastas have revived the African herbal tradition, giving rise to what they popularly refer to as the "Ital" [vital] tradition, which centers on the eating of herbs, grains, fruits and vegetables to the exclusion of meats, salts, artificial chemicals and sweeteners. ...The smoking of herbs for the Rastaman cannot be singled out from this herbal tradition as a whole and is very much a part of the same world movement now afoot towards greater wholesomeness and spiritual power based on ancient precepts". (Forsythe, 1999.) The use of ganja by the Rastafari is a logical extension of the striving for a more vital way of life and the preference for natural sources of food and medicine.

On the subject of 'ganja, the hola herb' it says in the first *Itations of Jamaica and I Rastafari* , "For the Rastafari, the use of Herb represents a sacrament of the Church Triumphant, serving creative thinking, relaxation and reasoning amongst the Brethren. It is interpreted as a Hola Herb given to man by the Creator for "the healing of the nations. ...The Herb, when smoked in a gathering, symbolizes the act of unification or "Inity" amongst those gathered together in the sight of the Most High Jah. It is accepted as binding the participants together in the fullness and powers of the Godhead thereby creating a vibrating flow of mutual Iditations [meditations] amongst those participating in this sacramental act." (Faristzaddi, 1987.)

Ganja herb is an intrinsic element of the mystical life of the Rastafari. It is used continually throughout day to day life and is a major part of the Nyahbinghi ritual experience. Ganja dissolves the barriers to "InI-consciousness", it aids the process of stepping up from one's normal state of consciousness and sense of self; it allows one to perceive one's true Self within the context of the Whole of the Iniverse, the 'One Love'. "It is believed among the brethren that during this state of spiritual uplift and heightened consciousness, they are in direct communion with Haile Selassie. This fosters a sense of togetherness, love and spiritual bonding among those present."(Reckford, 1998.).

To keep one's meditation flowing and one's focus ever on Jah Ras Tafari in these times, Rastafari burn the Hola Ishence (essence) regularly, sanctifying the physical body as a 'Temple of Fire'. At Nyahbinghi the Hola Herb must be present at the Altar and partaken of in the Inity of the congregation continually. It is seen as 'the healing of the nations', the 'Weed of Wisemind' and as the 'Burning Bush' and in smoking it (either through a water pipe or with a sprinkling of pure water on the prepared Herb) the Rasta mystic invokes the four elements Fire, Water, Earth and Air which are the Four Beasts who stand in the Throne Room of the Almighty I Jah. As the 'chalice', or bowl, of Herb is passed amongst InI it unifies and empowers InI intention while the smoke carries InI praises to Zion. By enhancing meditation and revealing the living Divine presence within each participant the Hola Herb has the same effect on the congregation as a whole. This is the Nyahbinghi sacrament of Communion, the spiritual fusion of man and Jah, of the lesser I with the greater I. For this moment the individual disappears and Divinity is experienced. 'As above, so below' is now no longer an enigmatic doctrine, it becomes a rather obvious statement of fact.

"By means of the hola herb which the Creator give man for meat, HIM servant separate himself from Babylon, even while in Babylon midst. Man purify man temple by burning this divine Ishence within. The herb is InI communion unto Jah, with Psalms, to drive out evil conception from man Living Church, and bar Babylon from re-entry. And tho' the System fight against herb, it cannot stop Rasta from using this divine purification to praise Jah Ras Tafari." (*Jahug,* vol. 2.)

"The Issembly is an occasion for the reinforcement of the value of the strict Ital 'livity' and precepts of Rastafari and for the purgation of Babylon's influence from one another's life". (Edmonds, 1998.) The Nyahbinghi gathering is the high point of the lives of many Rastas. Nyahbinghi spiritually energizes, like getting your spiritual battery super-charged. The uplift experienced at Nyahbinghi inspires and

encourages the constant meditation of the Inity of the
Iniverse, Jah Love, Haile Selassie I Jah Ras Tafari. Binghi
give I the strength to stay true upon the path of
Righteousness so that all 'the words of I mouth and the
meditations of I heart shall be acceptable in Jah sight'.

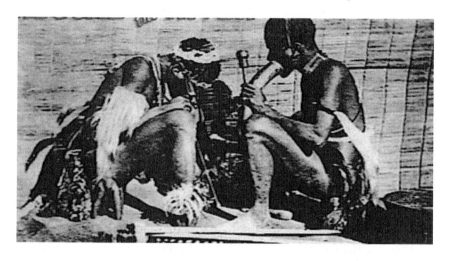

African herbsmen

'the healing of the nations'

VI. PRACTICE: Rastafari Livity

All Mystery Traditions agree upon the ultimate Unity of All and that experiencing and expressing that Unity can be more easily accomplished with a healthy body and a balanced mind. Different traditions offer different philosophies and practices to help achieve this experience and they may be judged by the fruit they bear. Violence, hatred, bigotry, prejudice, imbalance and discontent are the fruits of a poisoned tree, while peace, love, harmony, non-partiality, health and happiness are the signs of achievement.

"Livity" is the term used to indicate an uncompromising personal adherence to Rastafari precedents, precepts and principals. The purpose for and the function of Rasta livity is to bring one closer to the perfect Love and Iverstanding of Jah Ras Tafari and His natural laws of Creation. It is not a yardstick by which one can measure the piety or devotion of another. Selassie taught InI that, "As we do not practice or permit discrimination within our nation, so we oppose it wherever it is found. As we guarantee to each the right to worship as he chooses, so we denounce the policy which sets man against man on issues of religion".

"Rastafari livity is the natural God given life, it is an alternative to the decadent lifestyles of this age; Rastafari livity offers redemption and liberation from the outdoctrination and dead ways of the materialist society by showing the way to right living and the raising of consciousness above the level of the 'ego-life' which is centered in gross materialism. With the raising of consciousness comes spiritual awareness enabling one to realtruth [realize] the basic reality and oneness overtruthing [overlying] the manifested creation. The realtruezation [realization] of this basic reality or oneness with the spirit is the goal of human life and is referred to as self realtruezation, spiritual liberation, salvation or the Living Kingdom of Jah"; this Rasta's interpretation of livity is quoted from the second

Itations of Jamaica and I Rastafari. The concept of livity will have as many individual interpretations as adherents, but it is indispensable. If the symbols, myths and rituals are not vitalized by life-force they remain external and incomplete. Livity is the natural result of internalizing and assimilating the realization of the essential Truth within Rastafari.

The concept of livity is well grounded in both the teachings of Selassie and the Bible. "It is Our conviction that all the activities of the children of men which are not guided by the Spirit and counsel of God will bear no lasting fruit, they will not be acceptable in the sight of the LORD and will therefore come to naught as the Tower of Babel came to naught." These are the words of His Imperial Majesty Haile Selassie I, which no Rasta shall question. The Bible reminds us over and over that it is upon our thoughts and actions that we will be judged; "Blessed is the man that walketh not in the counsel of the ungodly, nor standeth in the way of sinners, nor sitteth in the seat of the scornful. But InI delight is in the law of Jah; and in His law doth InI meditate day and night. And InI shall be like the tree planted by the rivers of water, that bringeth forth InI fruit in due season. InI leaf also shall not wither; and whatsoever InI doeth shall prosper." (Ps. 1:1-3). Every one of us shall reap what we sow and Rastafari livity is a way to cultivate "good soil". "The seed is the Word of Jah", "on good soil are they, which in an honest and good heart, having heard the word, keep it, and bring forth fruit with patience." (Luke 8: 11, 15).

The Rastafarian term "Ital" means vital, it indicates purity and wholesomeness; being in a natural state, free from all artifice. For many Rastas, a major component of livity is the 'Ital' tradition, where it is reasoned "that the foods which we eat are the bearers of natural energies which are converted into physical forces and used by the material body in its daily functions. Many Rastafarians advocate the use of wholistic, non-processed foods of Mother Earth... Some brethren are wholly vegetarian, eating Ital food in its raw state; others prepare, cook and eat only Ital food, excluding all meat from their diet. Some eat Ital food and certain types of meat, while still others prefer the white meat of fish or poultry in preference to red meats". (Faristzaddi, 1987.) "Let not him that eateth despise him that eateth not; and let not him which eateth not judge him that eateth: for Jah hath received him." (Rom. 14:3). Clearly, it is the content of the heart and mind and not of the stomach by which we shall be judged. At the same time, a pure heart and a balanced mind do require a healthy body and Ital livity organically nourishes body, mind and soul.

The very strict code of livity originally forwarded by the Patriarchs of the Ancient Nyahbinghi Order required of a man that he:

- abide by the laws of H.I.M. Haile Selassie,
- abide with one woman, his Queen,
- be non-violent, non-abusive and non-partisan,
- be free from criminal activity,
- be free from whoredom, adultery and fornication,
- maintain Love and harmony at Nyahbinghi Issembly,
- avoid intimacy with whites,
- abide only with a Rastafari Queen and
- raise his youth as dreadlock Rastafari.

And the observances for a woman were that she:

- abide by the laws of H.I.M.,
- recognize her King (husband) as her head,
- avoid Nyahbinghi Issembly during menses,
- remain loyal to her King,
- be grounded at home, not a 'busy-body',
- not administrate around the Altar nor beat the harps at Nyahbinghi,
- cover her locks in Issembly,
- wear only modest apparel and
- fulfill the responsibility of teaching the youth.

On one hand, Rasta livity is a code of behaviors that one may adopt externally in order to effect desired changes internally, an expression of aspiration. On the other hand, it can also be the natural by-product of true spiritual development within the Rastafari tradition, an expression of achievement. Livity takes the Mysteries of Rastafari from the spiritual world of Truth, through the intellectual world of thought, and grounds them in the objective world of action.

Humankind has always sensed the existence of a whole greater than itself, of which it is part. And human beings have innately used the imaginative faculties to express their desire for and their achievement of communion with that whole. The Mystery traditions appeared as individuals discovered ways to experience the fullness of life and tried to share their insights. Rastafari is a modern Mystery tradition and proof of its validity is ascertainable to anyone of pure intention who perseveres with determination. By immersing in the symbols and myths of Rastafari, undergoing the transformational experience of Nyahbinghi and by nourishing body, spirit and mind through a natural livity, the Rastafari experience communion with the essential Unity of All, which is Jah.

Entrance to Nyahbinghi grounds

VII. THE BIBLE: Rastafari Scripture

Reading the Bible and smoking herb are mainstays of daily 'livity'. When Nyahbinghi Rastas read from scripture InI ad-lib an Iyaric translation while reading from a traditional translation of the Bible. So, a phrase such as "I will sing unto the LORD as long as I live; I will sing praise to my God while I have any being. My meditation of Him shall be sweet: I will be glad in the LORD" (Ps 104:33,34) might be read as "InI will chant unto JAH as long as InI live: InI will chant Ises unto Selassie I while InI have being. InI Iditation of HIM shall be sweet: InI will be glad in JAH Rastafari." With some practice this becomes second nature and a casual listener would assume that InI are reading from an actual Rastafari translation. A Rastafari translation of the Bible does not exist as yet and so, to provide the reader with a sense of this tradition, several of the most often cited Psalms are presented below in an 'Iyaric translation'.

When reading, not only is the Name of Haile Selassie interjected as synonymous with LORD or God, but other traditions need to be observed in order to appreciate the beauty of Iyaric. First, the use of "I" and/or "InI" is interjected at any appropriate opportunity, therefore 'forever' becomes 'forIver' (for-I-ver), 'praises' becomes 'Ises" and 'eternally' becomes 'Iternally'. The 'I' at the end of the Name Haile Selassie I is pronounced as 'I' and seldom as 'the first'; also an 'I' is often interjected between Haile and Selassie rendering the powerful invocation "Haile I Selassie I JAH Rastafari". The adjective 'him', wherever textually appropriate, is rendered 'H.I.M.' to reflect Selassie's title 'His Imperial Majesty'. When reciting scripture at Nyahbinghi the utterance of the Name 'JAH' usually elicits a spontaneous 'Rastafari!' from the congregation.

The same Rastaman reading the same passage twice may well not repeat it verbatim, maybe a 'JAH Rastafari' will be replaced by 'Haile I Selassie I' or an 'I' will come out as 'InI'. It is the spirit and meaning of the scripture that is tantamount, Iyaric is living poetry and not a rigid grammatical structure.

The Psalms reproduced here are those most commonly cited by the Rastafari. Some are used as a regular part of ritual (i.e. to open the tabernacle or to light the 'fire key'), some are seen as prophecy fulfilled in Haile Selassie I JAH Rastafari, and others are seen as scriptural validations of the Nyahbinghi Rastafari Tradition or as demonstrating the movement's roots in the Old Testament.

PSALM 1

Blessed is the man that walketh not in the counsel of
the ungodly,
nor standeth in the way of sinners, nor sitteth in the
seat of the scornful.
But InI delight is in the law of JAH; and in His law doth
InI meditate day and night.
And InI shall be like a tree planted by the rivers of
water, that bringeth forth InI fruit in due season; InI leaf
also shall not wither; and whatsoever InI doeth shall
prosper.
The ungodly are not so, but are like the chaff which the
wind driveth away.
Therefore, the ungodly shall not stand in the judgment,
nor sinners in the congregation of the righteous.
For JAH Rastafari Haile Selassie I knoweth the way of
the righteous; but the way of the ungodly shall perish.

PSALM 2

Why do the heathen rage and the people imagine a
vain thing?
The kings of the earth set themselves, and the rulers
take counsel together against JAH, and against His
anointed, saying, 'Let us break their bands asunder
and cast away their cords from us'.
He that sitteth in the heavens shall laugh; JAH
Rastafari shall have them in derision.
Then shall He speak unto them in His wrath and vex
them in His sore displeasure.
Yet have I set InI King upon InI hola hill of Zion.
InI will declare the decree: JAH hath said unto InI,
'Thou art I Son; this day have I begotten thee. Ask of I,
and I shall give thee the heathen for thine inheritance
and the uttermost parts of the earth for thy possession.
Thou shalt break them with a rod of iron; thou shalt
dash them in pieces like a potter's vessel'.

Be wise now therefore O ye kings: be instructed ye
judges of the earth.
Serve JAH Rastafari with fear and rejoice with
trembling. Kiss the Son lest He be angry and ye perish
from the way, when His wrath is kindled but a little.
Blessed are they that put their trust in Haile I Selassie I
JAH Rastafari.

PSALM 3

O JAH, how are they increased that trouble InI! Many
are they that rise up against InI. Many there be which
say of InI soul, 'There is no help for him in JAH'. Selah.
But Thou, O JAH, art a shield for InI; InI Glory and the
lifter up of InI head. InI cried unto Jah with InI
Word\Sound\Power and He heard InI out of His hola hill.
Selah.
InI laid down and slept; InI awakened; for JAH
sustained InI. InI will not be afraid of ten thousands of
people that have set themselves against InI round
about.
Arise O JAH, save InI, O I God: for Thou hast smitten
all InI enemies upon the cheek bone; Thou hast broken
the teeth of the ungodly.
Salvation belongeth unto Haile Selassie I JAH
Rastafari: Thy blessing is upon InI, Thy people. Selah.

PSALM 4

Hear InI when I call, O JAH of InI righteousness: Thou
hast enlarged I when InI was in distress; have mercy
upon I and hear InI prayer.
O ye sons of men, how long will ye turn InI glory into
shame? How long will ye love vanity and seek after
falsehood? Selah.
But know that JAH hath set apart him that is godly for
Himself: JAH will hear when InI call unto HIM.
Stand in awe and sin not; commune with InI own heart
upon InI own bed and be still. Selah.

Offer the sacrifices of righteousness and put trust in
JAH.
There be many that say, 'Who will show us any good?'
JAH, lift Thou up the Light of Thy Countenance upon
InI. Thou hast put gladness in InI heart more than in
the time that InI corn and wine increased.
InI will both lay down in peace and sleep: for Thou,
Haile Selassie I JAH Rastafari, only makest InI to dwell
in safety.

PSALM 5

Give ear to InI words, O JAH, consider InI meditation.
Hearken unto the voice of I cry, InI King and God: for
unto Thee will InI pray. InI voice shalt Thou hear in the
morning, O JAH; in the morning will InI direct I prayer
unto Thee and will look up.
For Thou art not a God that hath pleasure in
wickedness: neither shall evil dwell with Thee.
The foolish shall not stand in Thy sight: Thou hatest all
the workers of iniquity. Thou shalt destroy them that
speak leasing: JAH will abhor the bloody and deceitful
man.
But as for InI, I will come into Thy house in the
multitude of Thy mercy: and in Thy fear will InI worship
toward Thy Hola Temple.
Lead InI, O JAH, in Thy righteousness because of InI
enemies; make Thy way straight before InI face.
For there is no faithfulness in their mouth; their inward
part is very wickedness; their throat is in an open
sepulcher; they flatter with their tongue. Destroy Thou
them, O JAH, let them fall by their own counsels; cast
them out in the multitude of their transgressions; for
they have rebelled against Thee.
But let all those that put their trust in Thee rejoice: let
them ever shout for joy because Thou defendest them:
let them also that love Thy Name be joyful in Thee.

For Thou, Haile I Selassie I JAH Rastafari, wilt bless the righteous; with favour wilt Thou compass InI as with a shield.

PSALM 6

O JAH, rebuke InI not in Thine anger, neither chasten I in Thy hot displeasure. Have mercy upon InI, O JAH; for I am weak: O JAH, heal InI; for I bones are vexed. InI soul is also sore vexed: but Thou, O JAH, how long? Return, O JAH Rastafari, deliver InI soul: O save I for Thy Mercy's sake. For in death there is no remembrance of Thee: in the grave who shall give Thee thanks? I am weary with groaning; all the night make I I bed to swim; I watereth I couch with I tears. I eye is consumed because of grief; it waxeth old because of all I enemies. Depart from InI all ye workers of iniquity; for JAH hath heard the voice of InI weeping. JAH hath heard InI supplication; Haile Selassie I JAH Rastafari shall receive InI prayer. Let all InI enemies be ashamed and sore vexed: let them return and be ashamed suddenly.

PSALM 7

O JAH InI God, in thee do InI put I trust: save InI from all them that persecute InI, and deliver InI: Lest he tear InI soul like a lion, rending it in pieces, while there is none to deliver. O JAH Rastafari InI God, if InI have done this; if there be iniquity in I hands; if InI have rewarded evil unto him that was at peace with InI; yea, I have delivered him that without cause is I enemy: Let the enemy persecute InI soul, and take it; yea, let him tread down I life upon the earth and lay I honor in the dust. Selah.
Arise, O JAH Rastafari, in Thine anger, lift up Thyself because of the rage of InI enemies: and awake for InI to the judgment that Thou hast commanded. So shall

the congregation of the people compass Thee about: for their sakes therefore return Thou on high.

Haile Selassie I JAH Rastafari shall judge the people: judge InI, O JAH, according to InI righteousness and according InI integrity that is in InI. Oh let the wickedness of the wicked come to an end; but establish the just: for the righteous JAH trieth the hearts and reins.

InI defense is of JAH Rastafari which saveth the upright in heart. JAH judgeth the righteous and JAH is angry with the wicked every day.

If one does not repent, JAH will whet his sword: he hath bent his bow and made it ready. He hath also prepared the instruments of death; he ordaineth his arrows against the downpressers. Behold how he conceiveth evil, and is heavy with mischief, and bringeth forth falsehood. He made a pit, and digged it, and is fallen into the ditch which he made. His mischief shall return upon his own head, and his violent dealing shall come down upon his own pate.

InI will praise JAH according to his righteousness and will sing praise to the name of Haile Selassie I, Most High JAH Rastafari.

PSALM 9

InI will praise thee, O JAH Rastafari, with InI whole heart; InI will show forth all thy marvelous works. InI will be glad and rejoice in thee: InI will sing praise to thy name, O thou Most High Selassie I.

When InI enemies are turned back, they shall fall and perish at thy presence. For thou hast maintained I right and I cause; thou satest in the throne judging right. Thou hast rebuked the heathen, thou hast destroyed the wicked, Thou hast put out their name for Iver and Iver. The enemies are come to a perpetual end, ruins everlasting: and thou hast destroyed their cities; the very memory of them is perished with them.

But JAH Rastafari shall endureth forIver: he hath prepared his throne for judgment. And he shall judge the world in righteousness; he shall minister judgment to the people in uprightness.

JAH also will be a refuge for the downpressed, a refuge in times of trouble. And they that know thy name shall put their trust in thee: for thou, JAH Rastafari hast not forsaken them that seek thee.

Sing praises to Haile Selassie I which dwelleth in Zion: declare among the people his doings. For He who avenges blood remembereth the afflicted: He forgeteth not their cry.

Have mercy upon InI, O JAH; consider InI trouble which InI suffer of them that hate InI, Thou that liftest InI up from the gates of death: That InI may shew forth all Thy praise in the gates of the daughter of Zion: InI will rejoice in Thy salvation.

The heathen are sunk down in the pit that they made: in the net which they hid is their own foot taken. JAH is known by the judgment which He executeth: the wicked is snared in the work of his own hands. Higgaion. Selah.

The wicked shall be turned into hell and all nations that forget JAH. For the needy shall not always be forgotten: the expectation of the poor shall not perish forIver.

Arise, O JAH Rastafari; let not man prevail: let the heathen be judged in Thy sight. Put them in fear, O Haile I Selassie I JAH Rastafari: that the nations may know themselves to be but men. Selah.

PSALM 11

In JAH Rastafari put InI I trust: how say ye to InI soul, 'Flee as a bird to your mountain'? For, lo, the wicked bend their bow, they make ready their arrow upon the string that they may privily shoot at the upright in heart. If the foundations be destroyed, what can the righteous do? JAH is in His hola temple, Haile Selassie I's throne is in heaven: His eyes Ihold, His eyelids try the children of men. JAH trieth the righteous: but the wicked and him that loveth violence His soul hateth. Upon the wicked shall He rain snares, fire and brimstone and an horrible tempest: this shall be the portion of their cup.

For the righteous JAH Rastafari loveth righteousness; His Countenance doth Ihold the upright.

PSALM 20

JAH hear InI in the day of trouble; the name of Haile Selassie I defend InI; Send InI help from the sanctuary and strengthen InI out of Zion. Remember all InI offerings and accept InI burnt sacrifice, Selah.

Grant InI according to InI own heart and fulfill all InI plans. InI will rejoice in Thy victory and in the name of Haile Selassie I, InI will set up InI banner: JAH Rastafari fulfill all InI petitions.

Now knoweth InI that JAH saveth His anointed; He will hear InI from His hola heaven with the saving strength of His right hand.

Some trust in chariots, and some in horses: but InI will remember the name of Haile Selassie I JAH Rastafari, InI God. They are brought down and fallen: but InI are risen and stand upright. O JAH, grant InI victory: Let the King answer InI when InI call.

PSALM 24

The earth is JAH's and the fullness thereof; the world and they that dwell therein. For He hath founded it upon the seas and established it upon the floods. Who shall ascend into the hill of JAH? Or who shall stand in His hola place? He that hath clean hands and a pure heart; who hath not lifted up his soul unto vanity nor sworn deceitfully. He shall receive the blessing from JAH and righteousness from the God of InI salvation. This is the generation of them that seek thy face O Jacob. Selah.

Lift up your heads O ye gates and be ye lift up, ye Iverlasting doors; and the King of Glory shall come in. Who is this King of Glory? Haile Selassie I JAH Rastafari strong and mighty, JAH mighty in battle. Lift up your heads O ye gates; even lift them up ye Iverlasting doors; and the King of Glory shall come in. Who is this King of Glory? Haile Selassie I JAH of hosts, He is the King of Glory. Selah.

PSALM 66

Make a joyful noise unto JAH all ye lands: Sing forth the honor of His name: make His praise glorious. Say unto JAH, 'How terrible art Thou in Thy works! Through the greatness of Thy power shall Thine enemies submit themselves unto Thee. All the earth shall worship Thee and sing unto Thee; they shall sing unto Thy name.' Selah.

Come and see the works of JAH Rastafari: He is terrible in His doing toward the children of men. He turned the sea into dry land: InI went through the flood on foot: there did InI rejoice in HIM. He ruleth by His power forIver; His eyes Ihold the nations: let not the rebellious exhaust themselves. Selah.

O bless InI God, ye people, and maketh the voice of His praise to be heard: Which holdeth InI soul in life and suffereth not InI feet to be moved. For Thou, O JAH, hast proved InI: Thou hast tried InI as silver is tried. Thou broughtest InI into the net; Thou laidst affliction upon InI loins. Thou hast caused men to ride over InI heads; InI went through fire and through water: but Thou broughtest InI out into a wealthy place.

InI will go into Thy house with burnt offerings: InI will pay Thee InI vows, which I lips have uttered and I mouth hath spoken when InI was in trouble. InI will offer unto Thee burnt sacrifices of fatlings with the

incense of rams; InI will offer bullocks with goats.
Selah.
Come and hear, all ye that fear JAH, and InI will
declare what He hath done for I soul. I cried unto HIM
with I mouth and He was extolled with I tongue. If InI
regard iniquity in I heart, JAH will not hear InI. But
verily Haile Selassie I hath heard InI; He hath attended
to the voice of I prayer. Blessed be JAH Rastafari
which hath not turned away InI prayer nor His Mercy
from InI.

PSALM 72

Give the King Thy judgments, O JAH, and Thy
righteousness unto the King's son. He shall judge Thy
people with righteousness and Thy poor with judgment.
The mountains shall bring peace to InI and the little
hills by righteousness. He shall judge the poor of the
people; He shall save the children of the needy and
shall break in pieces the downpresser.
They shall fear Thee as long as the sun and moon
endure, throughout all generations.
He shall come down like rain upon the mown grass: as
showers that watereth the earth. In His days shall the
righteous flourish; and abundance of peace so long as
the moon endureth. He shall have dominion also from
sea to sea, and from the river unto the ends of the
earth. They that dwell in the wilderness shall bow
before HIM; and His enemies shall lick the dust.
The kings of Tarshish and of the isles shall bring
presents: the kings of Sheba and Seba shall offer gifts.
Yea, all the kings shall fall down before HIM. For He
shall deliver the needy when InI crieth; the poor also
and him that hath no helper. He shall spare the poor
and needy and shall save the souls of the needy. He
shall redeem InI soul from deceit and violence: and
precious shall InI blood be in His sight.

And He shall live, and to HIM shall be given the gold of
Sheba: prayer also shall be made for HIM Itinually;
and daily shall He be praised. There shall be an
handful of corn in the earth upon the top of the
mountains; the fruit thereof shall shake like Lebanon:
and they of the city shall flourish like grass of the earth.
His name shall endureth forIver: His name shall be
continued as long as the sun: and men shall call HIM
blessed.
Blessed be Haile I Selassie I JAH Rastafari, the God of
Israel, who only doeth wondrous things. And blessed
be His glorious name forIver: and let the whole earth
be filled with His Glory; Amen, and Amen.

PSALM 81

Sing aloud unto JAH InI strength: make a joyful noise
unto the God of Jacob. Take a psalm, and bring hither
the timbrel, the pleasant harp with the psaltery. Blow
up the trumpet in the new moon, in the time appointed,
on InI solemn feast day. For this was the statute for
Israel, and a law of the God of Jacob. This He
ordained in Joseph for a testimony, when he went out
through the land of Egypt: where InI heard a strange
language that InI overstood not.
I removed his shoulder from the burden: his hands
were delivered from the pots. Thou calledest in trouble,
and I delivered thee; I answered thee in the secret
place of thunder: I proved thee at the waters of
Meribah. Selah.
Hear, O I people, and I will testify unto thee: O Israel, if
thou wilt hearken unto I; There shall no strange god be
in thee; neither shalt thou worship any strange god. I
am JAH Rastafari thy God, which brought thee out of
the land of Egypt: open thy mouth wide, and I will fill it.
But I people would not hearken to I Voice; and Israel
would none of I. So I gave them up unto their own
heart's lust: and they walked in their own counsels. O

that I people had hearkened unto I, and Israel had walked in I ways! I should soon have subdued their enemies, and turned I hand against their adversaries. The haters of JAH Rastafari should have submitted themselves unto HIM: but their time should have endured forIver. He should have fed them also with the finest of the wheat: and with honey out of the rock should I have satisfied thee.

PSALM 91

He that dwelleth in the secret place of the Most High shall abide under the shadow of the Almighty I JAH Rastafari.
InI will say of JAH, 'He is I refuge and I fortress: InI God; in HIM will InI trust. Surely, He shall deliver InI from the snare of the fowler and from the noisome pestilence. He shall cover InI with His feathers and under His wings shalt InI trust: His truth shall be InI shield and buckler. InI shalt not be afraid for the terror by night; nor for the arrow that flieth by day; nor for the pestilence that walketh in the darkness; nor for the destruction that wasteth at noonday.
A thousand shall fall at InI side, and ten thousand at InI right hand; but it shall not come nigh InI. Only with InI own eyes shalt InI Ihold and see the reward of the wicked. Because InI hast made Haile Selassie I JAH Rastafari InI refuge, even the Most High for InI habitation; There shall no evil befall InI, neither shall any plague come nigh InI dwelling.
For He shall give His angels charge over InI to keep InI in all ways. They shall bear InI up in their hands, lest InI dash I foot against a stone. InI shall tread upon the lion and the adder: the young lion and the dragon shalt InI trample under feet. Because He set His Love upon InI and InI will answer HIM: InI will be with HIM in trouble; InI will deliver HIM and honor HIM. With long life shall InI satisfy HIM and shew HIM InI salvation.

PSALM 97

JAH Rastafari reigneth; let the earth rejoice; let the multitude of isles be glad thereof.

Clouds and darkness are round about HIM: righteousness and judgment are the habitation of His Throne. A fire goeth before HIM and burneth up His enemies round about. His lightnings enlighten the world: the earth saw and trembled.

The hills melted like wax at the presence of JAH, at the presence of Haile Selassie I, Lord of the whole earth. The heavens declare His righteousness and all the people see His Glory.

Confounded be all they that serve graven images, that boast themselves of idols: Worship HIM, all ye gods.

Zion heard and was glad; and the daughters of Judah rejoiced because of Thy judgments, O JAH. For Thou, JAH Rastafari, art high above all the earth: Thou art exalted far above all gods.

InI that loveth Haile Selassie hateth evil: He preserveth the souls of His saints; He delivereth InI out of the hand of the wicked. Light is sown for the righteous and gladness for the upright in heart.

Rejoice in Haile I Selassie I JAH Rastafari, ye righteous; and give thanks at the remembrance of His Holaness.

PSALM 101

InI will chant of mercy and judgment: unto Thee, O JAH, will InI chant. InI will behave wisely in a perfect way. O when wilt Thou come unto InI? InI will walk within InI gates with a perfect heart. InI will set no wicked thing before InI eyes: InI hate the work of them that turn aside; it shall not cleave unto InI.

Perverse thoughts shall depart from InI: InI will not know a wicked person. Whoso privily slandereth his neighbor, him will InI cut off: him that hath an high look and a proud heart will not InI suffer.

InI eyes shall be upon the faithful of the land, that they may dwell with InI: he that walketh in a perfect way, he shall serve InI.

He that worketh deceit shall not dwell within InI gates: he that telleth lies shall not tarry in InI sight. InI will early destroy all the wicked of the land; that InI may cut off all wicked doers from the City of JAH Rastafari.

PSALM 104

Bless the Lord, O I soul. Haile Selassie I JAH Rastafari, InI God, Thou art very great; Thou art clothed with honor and majesty. Who coverest Thyself with light as a garment: Who stretches out the heavens like a curtain: Who layeth the beams of His chambers in the waters: Who maketh the clouds His chariot: Who walketh upon the wings of the wind: Who maketh His angels spirits; His ministers a flaming fire: Who laid the foundations of the earth, that it should not be removed forIver.

Thou coveredest the earth with the deep as with a garment: the waters stood above the mountains. At Thy rebuke they fled; at the Voice of Thy thunder they hasted away. They go up by the mountains; they go down by the valleys unto the place which Thou hast founded for them. Thou hast set a bound that they may not pass over; that they turn not again to cover the earth.

He that sendeth the springs into the valleys, which run among the hills. They give drink to every beast of the field: the wild asses quench their thirst. By them the fowls of the heaven have their habitation, which sing among the branches.

He watereth the hills from His chambers: the earth is satisfied with the fruits of Thy works. He causeth the grass to grow for the cattle and *herb for the service of man*: that He may bring forth food out of the earth; and wine that maketh glad the heart of man and oil to make his face shine and bread which strengtheneth his heart. The trees of JAH are full of sap; the cedars of Lebanon, which He hath planted; Where the birds make their nests: as for the stork, the fir trees are her gates. The high hills are a refuge for the wild goats; and the rocks for the cronies.

He appointed the moon for seasons: the sun knoweth his going down. Thou makest darkness, and it is night: wherein all the beasts of the forest do creep forth. The young lions roar after their prey, and seek their meat from JAH. The sun ariseth, they gather themselves together and lay them down in their dens. Man goeth forth unto his work and to his labor until evening. O JAH Rastafari, how manifold are Thy Works! In wisemind hast Thou made them all: the earth is full of Thy riches.

So is this great and wide sea, wherein all things creeping innumerable, both small and great beasts. There go ships: there is that Leviathan, whom Thou hast made to play therein.

These wait all upon Thee; that Thou mayest give them their meat in due season. That Thou givest them, they gather: Thou openest Thy hand, they are filled with good. Thou hidest Thou face, they are troubled: Thou takest away their breath, they die, and return to their dust. Thou sendest forth Thy Spirit, they are created: and Thou renewest the face of the earth.

The Glory of JAH shall endureth forIver: Haile I Selassie I JAH Rastafari shall rejoice in His Works. He looketh on the earth and it trembleth: He toucheth the hills and they smoke.

InI will chant unto JAH as long as InI live: InI will chant Ises unto InI God while InI have being. InI meditation of HIM shall be sweet: InI will be glad in JAH Rastafari. Let the sinners be consumed out of the earth and let the wicked be no more. Bless JAH, O I soul. Praise InI His Imperial Majesty Haile I Selassie I JAH Rastafari.

PSALM 110

JAH sayeth unto InI Lord, 'Sit Thou at I right hand until I make Thine enemies Thy footstool.'
JAH shall send the rod of InI strength out of Zion: rule Thou in the midst of Thine enemies. Thy people shall be willing in the day of Thy Power, in the beauties of holiness from the womb of the morning: Thou hast the dew of Thy youth.
JAH hath sworn, and will not repent, *'Thou art a priest forIver after the Order of Melchizedek'*.
JAH at Thy right hand shall strike through kings in the day of His Wrath. He shall judge among the heathen, He shall fill the places with the dead bodies; He shall wound the heads over many countries. He shall drink of the brook in the way: therefore shall He lift up the head.

PSALM 121

InI will lift up I eyes unto the hills from whence cometh InI help. InI help cometh from JAH Rastafari which made heaven and earth. He will not suffer InI foot to be moved: He that keepeth InI shall not slumber. Ihold, He that keepeth Israel shall neither slumber nor sleep. JAH is InI keeper: Haile Selassie I is InI shade upon I right hand. The sun shall not smite I by day nor the moon by night. JAH shall preserve InI from all evil: He shall preserve InI soul. JAH Rastafari shall preserve InI going out and InI coming in from this time forth, and even forIver more.

PSALM 133

Ihold, how good and pleasant it is for brethren and sistren to dwell together in Inity! It is like the precious ointment upon the head, that ran down upon the beard, even Aaron's beard: that went down to the skirts of his garments.

As the dew of Hermon, and as the dew that descended
upon the mountains of Zion: for there Haile I Selassie I
JAH Rastafari commanded the blessing – even life
forIver more.

PSALM 149

Praise ye JAH Rastafari! Chant unto JAH a new song,
and His Ises in the congregation of saints. Let Israel
rejoice in HIM that made him: let the children of Zion
be joyful in InI King. Let InI praise His Name in the
dance: let InI chant Ises unto HIM with the timbrel and
harp. For JAH Rastafari taketh pleasure in His people:
He will beautify the meek with salvation.
Let the saints be joyful in glory: let InI chant aloud
upon InI bed. Let the Ises of JAH Rastafari be in InI
mouth and a two-edged sword in InI hand; to execute
vengeance upon the heathen, and punishments upon
the people; to bind their kings with chains, and their
nobles with fetters of iron; to execute upon them the
judgment written: this honor have all His saints. Praise
ye Haile Selassie I JAH Rastafari.

PSALM 151

HalleluJAH! A psalm of David, son of Jesse.
I was smaller than I brothers, youngest of I father's
sons. So he made I a shepherd for his sheep, a ruler
over his goats. I hands fashioned a pipe, I fingers a
lyre, and I glorified JAH.
I said to Iself, 'The mountains do not testify to HIM, nor
do the hills proclaim'.
So, echo I words, O trees, O sheep, I deeds!
Ah, but who can proclaim, who declareth the deeds of
JAH?
JAH Rastafari has seen all, heard and attended to
Iverything. He sent His prophet to anoint I, even
Samuel, to raise I up.

I brothers went forth to meet him: handsome of figure, wondrous of appearance, tall were they of stature, so beautiful their locks – yet JAH did not choose them. No, He sent and took I who followed the flock, and anointed I with the hola oil. He set I as a prince to His people, ruler over the children of His Covenant.

While Psalms figure prominently in the scriptural themes of Rastafari, there are other passages from other books which are fundamental to a full scriptural overstanding of Rastafari. Below is listed some of the biblical scriptures considered fundamental to the Mysteries of Nyahbinghi Rastafari:

<u>Old Testament</u>
Genesis 2:13
Leviticus 21:5-8
Judges 13:5
Jeremiah 23
Zechariah 2 / 6
Isaiah 9:6,7 / 11:1-5 / 30:17 / 43
Proverbs 22

<u>New Testament</u>
Matthew 12:42 / 21: 43,44 / 22: 41-46
John 1: 1-5 / 16
Acts 2: 29,30
I Timothy 6: 13-17
I John 4: 1-3
Hebrews 7 / 12: 2,3
Revelations 5: 1-5 / 10: 10-12, 17, 18 / 11: 3-6 / 14: 2, 3 / 19: 11-16

"And InI saw Zion opened and Ihold a white horse; and He that sat upon him was called Faithful and True, and in righteousness He doth judge and make war."
- Revelation 19:11

Bibliography

Atiba Alemu I., Jahson. 1994. *The Rastafari Ible.* Chicago: Frontline Int'l.

Barrett Sr., Leonard E. 1997. *The Rastafarians.* Boston: Beacon Press.

Brooks, Miguel F. 1995. *Kebra Negast.* Lawrenceville, NJ: Red Sea Press.

Campbell, Joseph. 1988. *The Power of Myth.* New York: Doubleday.

Charles, R.H. 1896. *The Book of the Secrets of Enoch.* Oxford: Clarendon Press.

Ras Iah C. *Jahug* Vol. II, Ed. II. London.

Denning & Phillips. 1986. *The Sword and The Serpent (Vol. II).* St. Paul: Llewellyn Pub.

Edmonds, Ennis B. 1998. "The Structure and Ethos of Rastafari". In *Chanting Down Babylon: The Rastafari Reader.* Philadelphia: Temple University Press.

Ehrman, Bart D. 2003. *Lost Christianities.* New York: Oxford.

Faristzaddi, Millard. 1987. *Itations of Jamaica and I Rastafari: The First Itation.* Miami: Judah Anbesa Int'l.

Faristzaddi, Millard. 1991. *Itations of Jamaica and I Rastafari: The Second Itation.* Miami: Judah Anbesa Int'l.

Forsythe, Dennis. 1999. *Rastafari.* New York: One Drop Books.

Godwin, Joscelyn. 1981. *Mystery Religions.* New York: Harper & Rowe.

Hall, Manly P. 1988. *The Secret Teachings of All Ages.* Los Angeles: Philosophical Research Society.

Laurence, Richard. 1883. *The Book of Enoch the Prophet.* London: Wm. Clowes & Sons.

Lewis, Nabi Moshe Y. 1993. *Ancient Mysteries of Melchizedek.* Queens, N.Y.: D & J Books.

Reckford, Verena. 1998. "From Burru Drums to Reggae Riddims: The Evolution of Rasta Music" in *Chanting Down Babylon: The Rastafari Reader.* Philadelphia: Temple University Press.

Regardie, Israel. 2001. *The Tree of Life – 3rd ed.* St. Paul: Llewellyn Pub.

Savishinsky, Neil J. 1998. "African Dimensions of the Rastafarian Movement" in *Chanting Down Babylon: The Rastafari Reader.* Philadelphia: Temple University Press.

Taylor, Thomas. (translator). 1984. Iamblichus. *On the Mysteries.* San Diego: Wizards Bookshelf.

Ras Bongo Thyme. *Jahug* Vol. II, Ed. II. London.

CPSIA information can be obtained at www.ICGtesting.com
Printed in the USA
LVOW04s0251190515

439006LV00025B/435/P